UNTHINKABLE

UNTHINKABLE

The culture and politics
of getting innovation wrong

Tom Hopkins

Edited by Paul Dawson

New York

UNTHINKABLE

The culture and politics of getting innovation wrong

Published in New York, New York, by Morgan James Publishing. Morgan James and The Entrepreneurial Publisher are trademarks of Morgan James, LLC. www.MorganJamesPublishing.com

The Morgan James Speakers Group can bring authors to your live event. For more information or to book an event visit The Morgan James Speakers Group at www. TheMorganJamesSpeakersGroup.com.

ISBN 978-1-63047-483-6 paperback
ISBN 978-1-63047-485-0 ebook
Library of Congress Control Number: 2014919412

A **free** eBook edition is available with the purchase of this print book.

CLEARLY PRINT YOUR NAME ABOVE IN UPPER CASE

Instructions to claim your free eBook edition:
1. Download the BitLit app for Android or iOS
2. Write your name in **UPPER CASE** on the line
3. Use the BitLit app to submit a photo
4. Download your eBook to any device

Front cover image, 'Company Hierarchy' and 'Endless Organizational Consensus' by Hugh MacLeod, © Gaping Void

Einstein: The Library of Congress

David Brent: Copyright © BBC

Josh Lyman: Licensed by Warner Bros. Entertainment Inc. All rights reserved.

Remaining images: © Fluxx Ltd

Copy editing:
Lisa Carden

In an effort to support local communities and raise awareness and funds, Morgan James Publishing donates a percentage of all book sales for the life of each book to Habitat for Humanity Peninsula and Greater Williamsburg.

Get involved today, visit
www.MorganJamesBuilds.com

Habitat
for Humanity®
Peninsula and
Greater Williamsburg
Building Partner

For my girls:
Peggy, Zahra and Ella

Table of Contents

	Foreword	ix
	Acknowledgements	xiii
Chapter 1	Introduction	1
Chapter 2	When a Revolution is Required	6
Chapter 3	Myth and Magic	15
Chapter 4	Innovation Today	26
Chapter 5	Driving Forces	53
Chapter 6	What Makes Products Successful?	72
Chapter 7	Making the Unthinkable Thinkable	79
Chapter 8	Running an Innovation Process	119
Chapter 9	Tomorrow	157
	References	161

Foreword

Looking back, boo.com was the start of it all. Not many books will begin like that.

But boo.com was the peak of the first dot.com bubble, and that — in turn — was when the world of business which we all occupy changed forever.

Before boo and the boom, the comings and goings of big companies were less dramatic — more like the drifting of continents than the surging of armies.

Now, 15 years later, we can see that tech didn't just change our lives; it also changed forever the pace of businesses.

Seemingly overnight, new markets would displace old. A company you'd never heard of would get a billion-dollar valuation on a stock market you'd also never heard of. Your kids would introduce you to a million-person online phenomenon. Bookshelves filled with apocalyptic business tomes. CEOs had to have an innovation agenda.

Tom was with me back then too. We were working at the heart of the new beast — in the best digital agency in London — learning and then deploying the craft of this new age to our clients' advantage.

And then our industry, like those of our clients, became violently different. And so the idea came to do something new. And not just once. We'd try to do something new every day. We'd start an innovation agency. At the time, that was a radical thought.

And that was what Fluxx was all about. Find a client that wants to change, that knows that today's certainties aren't good enough anymore, and help them find their tomorrow.

We've all read the great books on innovation — Christensen, Kelley, Reis — but Tom's book is different. He has set out to help you understand the 'why' of when innovation works well and when it doesn't from a human point of view.

This is not theory; it is a chronicle of the realities of big businesses. And having read the book, you should be armed with a deeper understanding of why no single innovation approach will fit every company. In turn, this will help you find the right way for your organisation.

For years, amid many successes, each of us at Fluxx has experienced the painful realities of companies attempting new things. We've seen the full range of tortuous processes companies follow to create new products and services. We've helped companies build some great products in this time, and we're lucky to have been involved with some brilliant brands and individuals in doing so. But just as often, we've seen great ideas turned terrible by the execution or the politics, and seen companies invest huge amounts of time and money in building products that customers simply don't want.

We'd rather not work this way and here, in this book, Tom has set out to help us all understand why organisations hit the buffers with innovation, and to identify practical changes that can be made to approaching innovation which will make new products much more likely to succeed. Of course, you shouldn't expect easy or obvious answers. Many elements of this new approach are more challenging than the old ways, and require significant rethinking and retraining. Often they require major changes in behaviour, overcoming previous instincts and many years of ingrained habits. Much like kicking any habit, the changes are easy to say yet hard to do.

This is not for the faint of heart. Rather, we at Fluxx hope to work with a new generation of leaders who would prefer to go out on a limb than to watch projects — and even companies — fail through a lack of momentum and innovation.

Here you won't find a single approach. Instead, as part of the new generation of innovator, you will be armed with the understanding to diagnose your own organisation, and give you the confidence and belief to make a change. This change will allow your company to think what might previously have seemed unthinkable and — in doing so — achieve what may previously have been unachievable.

—**Richard Poole**
Founder, Fluxx

Acknowledgements

When we first set out to write the book, I expected it would have 25 authors — the team at Fluxx — and one editor (me). As it worked out, it has had one author and 25 editors.

Each of the team has contributed ideas, case histories, anecdotes, better thinking, and even a couple of jokes; they've picked nits, rewritten pieces, made suggestions and generally made the book much better than it was when I started.

Like much of what we do, it has reminded me of the unassailable privilege of working with such a smart bunch of like-minded individuals.

The mistakes are mine, the credit is theirs.

There is one editor I must thank in particular. Paul Dawson, one of Fluxx's founders, has spent many days poring over the text, painstakingly ensuring that it stands up to the scrutiny of the real world and accurately reflects the best thinking of Fluxx. For joining me so closely on the incredible journey of turning these ideas into a single tome, I will forever be in his debt.

—**Tom Hopkins**

Chapter 1

Introduction

*'Embracing the status quo as an operating principle
is going to put you on a collision course with time.'*
—**Howard Shultz**[1]

When Kodak filed for bankruptcy protection in January 2012, it would have been easy to assume that the company had been the victim of more nimble, more digital innovators who had created exciting new products which stole consumer attention and market share.

In fact, for the most part, the innovations that took away Kodak's hugely lucrative film and processing business came from the company's own research and development labs.

---

1   http://www.letgoandlead.com/howard-schultz/

Kodak invented the digital camera and for a period became market leader, notably building Apple's first *QuickTake* camera. However, within just a few years, the business was unable to compete. There was a distinct failure to create sufficiently compelling products, and the company never really escaped its history of chemistry and paper so that it could profit in the new market of unlimited digital images.

Is Kodak alone in this? Hardly. Think of Xerox — inventor of many of the elements of the modern PC. HMV in the UK and Tower Records in the US were, for a period, amongst the biggest players in digital downloads. Microsoft produced the first commercially available tablet computers and many of the world's first smart phones. Look inside virtually any failing, failed or declining business from the last decade and you are likely to find the origins of the innovation with which it is now battling.

In each case, it is not the idea — which may be quite simple — but rather the ability to bring the product to market in a compelling way which the incumbent fails to grasp.

This breakdown in imagination, whilst not deliberate, is nothing less than a by-product of the company's success. Once a business learns how to do one thing well, it seems, it learns to actively mobilise against the forces trying to do something new.

Often it is only when the company's current product line is in severe decline that there is enough energy to effect a change.

How will you react when this happens to you — when you find your business model no longer delivers the returns your shareholders and stakeholders expect? Will you really try to do something new? Or will you seek out other options: perhaps cutting costs or buying a competitor to keep the show on the road for a little longer?

This is the nightmare scenario, the ever-present fear of every CEO. This is the Unthinkable — that which we dare not contemplate. Our

businesses are structured as if to avoid this very question. But it is —
equally — inevitable. We know it's coming sooner or later. So why do
so many of us obstinately refuse to think about such an eventuality until
it is too late?

Changing this bias — making the unthinkable thinkable — requires
people who have spent many years believing one thing to suddenly
believe in another. And that transition will feel like the end of the world.
Because it is — the end of one world and the beginning of a new one.

Whichever business you are in, the end of the world is coming. So,
prepare now.

It takes a certain type of leadership to make that kind of
transformation happen, to make it something staff, investors, partners
and customers can embrace.

Yet, the largest and best-run companies are often the ones that
find it hardest to adapt and to grasp new opportunities, to raise their
game against the mostly obvious threats posed by new technologies and
competitors.

Of course, the opportunity is for incumbents to free themselves
of this suicidal trait. If only the restraining factors could be released;
established businesses have many advantages in bringing new products
to market including reach, brand, capital and expertise. Small companies
are often more nimble than large ones. But not always. Apple is not a
small company.

At Fluxx, our innovation consultancy, we've sometimes said that we
help big companies act like startups. But the truth is we want more than
that. We want big companies to act like super-startups — able to do so
much more with their ideas than the next bunch of students in a garage
or back-bedroom.

It has been our mission to work with some of the world's largest
companies to do exactly that — to unleash the power of large brands
to break down these barriers to new directions, ideas and markets.

We have established tools and techniques which make a radical difference. In changing attitudes and expectations, we have been able to make the act of disruptive innovation possible in some of the world's biggest and most conservative businesses.

In the chapters that follow, we will describe the journey we have followed in solving these problems.

First, we will debunk some of the myths which surround innovation and business development practice: the post-rationalised stories management tells itself, the fake histories of the case study, the desire to keep telling the fable of the leader who can succeed by breaking all the rules.

Next, we will examine some of the counterproductive behaviours we have seen in companies that try, and fail, to do new things, and their deep-seated causes.

At the heart of the problem there is a simple truth: too often management teams are dysfunctional about the future, choosing today's certainties over tomorrow's challenges, even when the profits and promise of tomorrow are likely to evaporate without changes. The status quo is preferred, creating a short-sightedness about trouble soon at hand, and a preference for continuing on today's course, even if it leads nowhere.

Finally, we will lay out what we have learnt about how businesses can successfully do new things.

By turning on its head much of the macho business thinking of today, we have found new ways to construct and manage innovation programmes which deliver real value over business shamanism. These are designed around how individuals and groups really work both in your businesses and in your markets; and they give innovation leaders a realistic way to keep the innovation effort on track.

We know our techniques work, because we have seen them work many times within our clients' companies. They will work for your business too if you can stick to the principles we outline below.

Once we have understood what is really happening when companies appear to turn against innovation — like antibodies attacking a virus — we will look at what solutions are available to help companies do new things. Which structures work and which don't? How do we incentivise and manage amid uncertainty? Does it have to be so stressful? How should executive teams be managed in the process? How do we best ensure that we learn from our mistakes?

What we will find is that this is a subject area unnecessarily full of myth and magic. Many of the answers are common sense; it's just not the same type of common sense you need for the day-to-day management of firms.

Telling tales

Throughout this book, we will attempt to bring to life what we have learnt through our own research and case histories. Often these will need to be obfuscated. Names and circumstances will be changed to protect the innocent — those within companies who did the right thing, or tried to, and still can't talk in public about their unthinkable actions.

Indeed, it is ironic that the stories which give the truest picture of how businesses adapt to change are rarely the stories which are told. As we discuss later, the art of writing case histories has evolved to a degree where they are no longer works of non-fiction.

We'd love to hear your stories and experiences too. Please do visit unthinkable.info to give us your feedback on anything you have read here.

Chapter 2

When a Revolution
is Required

We constantly hear that companies must innovate or die. In the UK, of the 100 companies that made up the FTSE 100 in 1984, only 24 remain today. And there's little doubt that the message has got through. Innovation is on the mind of any self-respecting CEO. Twenty-eight per cent of US business schools use the word, or a derivative thereof, in their mission statement while 43 per cent of US businesses have a 'chief innovation officer'.[2] Amazon used the word 'innovation' 3,190 times on its investor relations site alone.[3]

2 http://www.smartplanet.com/blog/business-brains/is-8216innovation-now-the-most-overused-word-in-business/24475
3 Fluxx internal research, September 2013.

It would be easy to get the impression that somehow, merely shoehorning this magic word into your job title or company description will make a difference. Recently, for example, there has been a trend whereby design agencies disappear one day and reappear the next as 'innovation' agencies. We're sure this is good (if transient) marketing, and it may even be motivational for the staff of these firms. However, it has also continued the long-running devaluation of the currency of that most overused word.

Even before innovation was bandied around to this degree, we found it awkward. It is simultaneously too broad and too narrow to describe the sorts of changes that we think are important for business. It's too broad because innovation could mean any change — no matter how small. Adding a company Twitter feed may — for many — be innovation but it's unlikely to add much value unless it comes with a corresponding change in attitude. And it's too narrow because a there is a kind of stigma around what happens when innovation initiatives fail and, frankly, around the sort of people who are involved in failed innovation initiatives.

Say the word 'innovator' and the mind naturally drifts to the likes of Einstein and Edison. Say the phrase 'innovation manager' and the image conjured up is of a middle-aged middle manager not in the prime of their career and who spends too much time at conferences. The innovation office, all too often, is the one next to the door.

We need to rid ourselves of these associations and hype so that we can focus on the types of innovation that really transform businesses. From our experience, the more extreme types of innovation can be very hard for businesses to execute effectively. For staff who are used to one thing, a sudden and complete change of tack is a real challenge. And so it is likely to be resisted.

We'll call these major changes 'revolutionary innovations', 'revolutionary businesses' or just 'revolutions', as opposed to 'normal businesses' or 'normal innovations'.

This is not a derogatory distinction. The world of business is built by day-to-day or 'normal' business managers; inventing the trains is one thing, getting them to run on time is what makes them useful. However, to find the next 'big thing' means looking outside the toolset of 'normal' management.

2.1 Defining 'normal' innovation

It's worth looking, briefly, at some of the huge range of activities that make up normal innovation:

- Improving existing business processes
  - ◊ Fine-tuning an existing process — the improved efficiencies that businesses need to find year in, year out. This could include anything from improving the quality of materials or boosting morale on the production line to finding a new way to take products to market, or incentivising sales teams.
  - ◊ More radical approaches to cost saving — like moving your factories to Taipei, or adopting lean approaches like agile or Six Sigma.

◊   Creating a whole new way to get things done — the way CAD changed manufacturing processes or desktop publishing changed newspaper production.

• Taking existing products to new markets
     Whether it's selling into a new market (e.g. starting to export your product to the States) or to a new demographic (e.g. selling Diet Coke to men through the Coke Zero brand), the ability to rethink proposition, marketing and application can be hugely demanding.

• Marketing products in new ways
     ◊   Using a content- or social media-driven marketing approach to offer a wider appeal.
     ◊   Creating multiple price tiers and product configurations.

• Adding new promotional packages — free trials, etc.

• Reconfiguring freemium models

The list goes on…

2.2 So what's revolutionary, then?

That's when we try to think up entirely new products for existing markets (e.g. Peppa Pig toys are sold to the same markets as Peppa Pig cartoon content), or when we try to find new products for new markets (such as when Starbucks convinced a nation of tea lovers that they couldn't do without their daily latte, or when Apple decided it would enter the music business).

Just because something is revolutionary for *your* business doesn't mean it has never been done before. But it does mean that it is new territory for you and those around you.

And what we know for sure is that while existing teams can often deliver 'normal' innovation — especially of the incremental kind — they struggle to deliver on 'revolutionary' invention. The teams at the coalface when it comes to operating today's products are almost always the best placed to find efficiencies and make recommendations for making those products better. In their book *The Idea-Driven Organization*,[4] Alan Robinson and Dean Schroeder argue that 80 per cent of the value that is delivered in terms of operational improvement comes from grass roots ideas. However, and maybe because of how close they are to today's operations, these teams often struggle to find the next product that may take the market by storm.

2.3 Why is this?

By necessity, the individuals involved in everyday ('normal') business are relentlessly focused on repeatability. Goals in these teams can be expressed in terms of results, so if a team is producing ten units per person per hour, a good performance is to make 11, a bad performance is to make nine. In addition, the teams must be motivated by quality of output and consistency. Managers have a relatively well-understood yardstick for performance, and staff can judge their own performance reasonably well. Targets in this arena are based on results and, thus, staff can easily be incentivised to keep output and quality high.

The 'normal' business is what Govindarajan and Trimble call the 'performance engine'[5] and a constant stream of 'normal' innovations can be made more likely by providing staff with autonomy, knowledge and space to make improvements. For example, companies might rotate staff through various roles to broaden their experience, could incentivise performance-improving initiatives, hold all-staff meetings to surface appropriate ideas or add a measure to incentives around the improvement of quality.

---

4   Robinson, A. and Schroeder, D. 2014. *The Idea-Driven Organization: Unlocking the Power in Bottom-up Ideas*. San Francisco: Berrett-Koehler.

5   Govindarajan, V. and Trimble, C. 2010. *The Other Side of Innovation: Solving the Execution Challenge*. Cambridge, MA: Harvard Business School Press.

In a sense, this conclusion — that existing teams are unlikely, by themselves, to be able to get the company doing new things or doing things in entirely new ways — is a shame. Clearly, for company leaders this would be both less risky (as it would not involve bringing in people they don't know) and potentially less expensive.

However, as we'll see in subsequent chapters, delivering more than incremental improvements will require a different approach; it demands new skills, new ways of managing and rewarding, and new ways of understanding success.

The next time you hear a management guru tell you that 'everyone in the company is responsible for innovation', ask them to explain the numerous examples of people at all levels who have to leave a business in order to create its next disruptive competitor, and the scarcity of organisations that have created a revolutionary product from a shop-floor-led approach.

2.4 The structure of business revolutions

The language we are using here to describe innovation activities is not original. In fact, we've borrowed 'normal' and 'revolutionary' from a highly influential American philosopher and historian of science, Thomas Kuhn, author of *The Structure of Scientific Revolutions* (1962), who caused many to rethink their assumptions about how the world of science really works.

For the most part,[6] people have a lot of faith in scientists and in the sanctity of the scientific method. That is to say, they believe that when scientists are presented with evidence that a scientific theory is incorrect or incomplete, that they will abandon the theory. Let's say that science tells us that emus are physically incapable of flight. One flying emu might be seen as a freak or a hoax, but once we've observed ten or 100

---

6   http://www.scientificamerican.com/article.cfm?id=in-science-we-trust-poll

soaring through the skies, we all agree it is time to revisit the theory on emus being unable to fly.

What Kuhn did was to look back at where there had been major revolutions in scientific thinking — the notion that the earth wasn't flat, that it wasn't at the centre of the universe, that planets do not have circular orbits and so on — and examined what really happened. What he found was that evidence did *not* tend to invalidate well-established theories. Rather, faith in prevailing scientific norms was so strong that anomalous (incompatible) results would often be dismissed as erroneous or explained away by complex extensions to the existing frameworks.

Take the well-known example of the elliptical orbits of planets. At the time of Kepler, the belief that planetary orbits are circular wasn't just popular, it wasn't even just a scientific 'fact'; it was a truth from the works of Aristotle, as much based on the philosopher's convictions as it was on scientific study.

To question this belief was virtually blasphemous. And so scientists would come up with other explanations for the observations they had made of planetary motion — such as the existence of other planets which could not be seen.

This is what Kuhn refers to as 'normal science'. During such phases, it is the (unspoken) job of the scientist to act within a well-established framework or paradigm. This is not to say that normal science is somehow wasteful or misleading. A lot of progress can be made in working in this way. After all, some coherent framework is always required to work in, and the work that scientists do still helps us to understand and — perhaps more importantly — predict the world.

Eventually, however, if evidence of anomalies continues to mount, a new framework may be proposed which will effectively oust the previous framework. Kuhn's analysis of this sort of change is the origin of the term 'paradigm shift'. It is what Kuhn refers to as 'revolutionary' science (Galileo's heliocentricity, Kepler's elliptical orbits, Einstein's theory of relativity and so on). Revolutions in science are rarer occurrences which happen during periods of upheaval. They require brave pioneers, they change the context for everyone, and they require other scientists to reconsider all of the work they have been doing. Eventually, the new paradigm will be able to explain more observations, more coherently than the previous paradigm.

However, in the shorter term, it may appear to have as many holes as the old framework, since it will require a lot of 'new', 'normal' science to rewrite the science text books under the new paradigm.

We think this relatively well-understood (although still contested) theory for scientific knowledge has plenty of parallels in the worlds of business in which we operate. For our purposes, the *normal* activity is the day-to-day operation of the business. The *revolutionary* activity is when businesses want to do entirely new things.

What we have perceived (as both consultants and as employees of large and small companies alike) — and as you'll have gathered by now — is that businesses are not very good at doing genuinely new things even when they are very good at carrying out their main business.

The reasons for this bias are subtle and hard to break. So, when businesses need to change or need to do new things, they are essentially trapped between two unpalatable options: do something uncomfortable and risky, or stay where it is comfortable and run the risk of obsolescence.

The challenge is to understand the factors that encourage this fundamental weakness and look at what we can do to make the 'unthinkable' change acceptable just as ground-breaking scientists must discard the paradigms of the previous generation.

2.5 Only when revolutions are required

And so, in this book, we will focus on where revolutions are required and, consequently, we will more than likely help people seeking new, breakthrough products or services. Things designed to make the competition sit up and pay attention.

And what we will see is that for revolutionary innovation to succeed, it is often the deep-seated structures inside the companies themselves which will need to change. The deadlock we want to break is the one where companies know that their current proposition (their products and services) will not provide them with a long-term reason to exist, and yet they decide, for whatever reason, to stick with them anyway.

In a world where staying still is the same as going backwards, and most investors demand a steady stream of year-on-year improvements, the need to constantly enter new markets, with new technology and new value propositions, is intense.

Getting to the next proposition, especially when the current one is working, is extremely challenging and will force companies to find a different sort of leader, one who can break out of the mould of 'innovation manager' and break away from the skills we associate with that: predictability, a keen ability to take credit for things, a sort of gung-ho self-confidence and the ability to sell ideas to other executives.

Chapter 3

Myth and Magic

Once we have understood what is really happening when companies appear to turn against revolutionary innovation, we will look at some solutions that can really help companies do new things. Which structures work and which don't? How do we incentivise and manage amid uncertainty? Does it have to be so stressful? How should executive teams be managed in the process? How do we best ensure that we learn from our mistakes?

What we will find is that this is a subject area unnecessarily full of myth and magic.

3.1 Myth: Everyone loves innovation

Setting out on a search for people who are innovation-averse is likely to be a fruitless task. Ask anyone about the importance of innovation and you'll see that you've found the rarest of topics — something that everyone agrees on.

Like mother's milk and apple pie, new is universally a Good Thing. Much better than old. And you'd be crazy not to be all for it. But asking if people are in favour of innovation is not really the right question. Instead we should ask: 'What do you want more than innovation?'

In reality, how many people really went to work for a twenty-year-old company with thousands of staff in order to do *new* things? How many people really ask questions in job interviews about how often their prospective employer completely changes direction? How many managers really relish rethinking how they report their successes and failures?

Choosing innovation makes the employee's career path much less certain. And, although many employees might understand the need to change, few will wholeheartedly push for that change to happen. Faced with important uncertainty or unimportant certainty, many will choose the latter.

3.2 Myth: Innovation can be made predictable

We've all watched enough TED (Technology, Entertainment and Design) talks to know that the brave innovator's story normally involves lots of uncertainty and risk. This is indeed inherent in doing new things — as every five-year-old knows.

Yet, companies with a 'macho' management culture, in particular, often place a strong emphasis on the apparent ability to predict the future, sometimes in the same breath as praising thinking 'outside the box'. These companies want to have their cake and eat it.

By valuing intuitive prediction over continual learning, companies create a culture where failure is likely to be delayed, more expensive and less productive.

The same management guru who is telling you about everyone in your business being an innovator probably also likes to talk about processes for making innovation more predictable. Like their shareholders in turn, these companies would love to find a predictable method of innovating, a method for creating sure-fire winners every time.

But if we try to introduce the predictability of regular management to innovation, we will only drag out failure. When we incentivise a particular skill — such as predicting the future — you can guarantee that people will start trying to deliver it and demonstrate it. And, thus, energy is expended on making impossible forecasts rather than on trying to find and evaluate ideas. In fact, the company has scored an own goal by creating a culture where staff are actively dis-incentivised from either trying new things or learning from their experiences.

3.3 Myth: Imagination is the key to innovation

There is a popular misconception that the hardest part of innovation, the most important job for the innovator, is coming up with great ideas. In books, and on TV, innovation is about the spark, about having an amazing idea. It's a process that takes place in the mind of the inventor.

As noted above, talk about innovators and the imagination springs to a brooding but primly-dressed gentleman, perhaps Edison or Tesla, or someone with crazy hair and wild eyes, perhaps Einstein or Doc Brown from *Back to the Future*. They have big brains, are buzzing with ideas and can't tie their shoelaces for the excitement this causes, all of which can result in disappointment when we actually start doing innovation for a job, in offices, with people who wear suits. It also conceals the key fact that the having of ideas is just one — admittedly important — part of the innovation process.

An innovation team looking to actually create something of value must be able to quickly understand the potential of ideas, and develop them so that they clearly resolve a customer challenge or create a new opportunity. The team must be able to figure out the commercial and technical realities of the product, as well as how to explain it to customers in a way which can be clearly understood — and which makes them want to spend their hard-earned money on it.

A successful innovation team must have all this nous, as well as the ability to actually make the product good. Sparky creativity alone is nothing without a more practical pair of hands to make sure ideas are related to the market, and still nothing without the careful guidance to execute the ideas effectively, keeping the original customer value proposition alive in the process.

3.4 Magic: The misdirection of success stories

In TV drama *The West Wing*, Josh Lyman, Deputy Chief of Staff to the US President, is talking to the Surgeon General of the United States who has publicly expressed her reservations about the legal status of marijuana. Josh points out that a very low proportion of Americans

(23 per cent) are in favour of decriminalisation. The Surgeon General replies that the figure is much higher if you limit the sample to those under 30. Josh replies: 'Well that's a shock. Did you know the number gets even higher than that if you limit the polling sample to Bob Marley and the Wailers?' (Season 2, Episode 15: 'Ellie'.)

Put like this, the absurdity of selecting only those examples that meet the criteria you are trying to test seems obvious and easily avoided.

However, it is exactly this effect — 'selection bias' — which has led to many of the most enduring myths about innovation practice.

Over and over again, we have heard companies follow this syllogism: Company X (Dropbox, Apple, etc) does its development, marketing and so on in this way and is very successful. We want to do our development, marketing and so on in the same way (so that we are successful too).

Ostensibly, it's a seductive argument but there is a snag: the sample size of companies that 'do X' has been reduced to one or two successful firms and the research has then been used to conclude that those businesses are successful. We have no way of knowing, however, how many other companies have 'done X' and failed.

Perhaps the most common anguished cry for innovators in recent times has been: 'How can I be like Instagram?' This strikes us as a very odd question. Fundamentally, what Instagram did was build an attractive iOS app which allowed users to apply effects to their iPhone pictures and to share them. The company certainly captured the imagination of iPhone users, built an app that was intrinsically viral and well designed, and have been hugely successful (they had 30 million registered users when they were sold to Facebook in 2012 for $1bn). So, of course, they are a popular role model for other startups wanting to make $1bn. But the question 'How can I be like Instagram?' is unhelpful because if we spend our time looking only at successful startups, we will forget to include the luck factor in our calculations, since we have already selected a bunch of companies who have clearly been pretty lucky in some regard. There are tens, if not hundreds, of businesses that do what Instagram does but have neither 30 million users nor $1bn of Facebook's money.

A similar, and very human, phenomenon is the desire to listen to stories about successful companies which follow a narrative structure that wouldn't be out of place in a pre-schooler's reading book.

As the great planner Stephen King describes in a 1960s paper, the typical form of case histories is marvellously abridged:

'[...] the usual sort of agency case history in which our immaculate heroes proceed, without hesitation, from brilliant analysis to startling conclusion and in the final frames stride into the sunset pursued by pathetic bleats of gratitude from their half-witted clients.'[7]

We see the same behaviour from businesses when they describe their early years, or a particular breakthrough moment. Of course, if you are writing for an annual report, or an autobiography, there is a strong incentive to remove the bits that don't appear clear-headed and decisive. This leaves readers forced to believe that the leader in question is some kind of super-human savant, never erring from the path of rational thought, able to foresee not just the running of their own business but even the future desires of their customers and otherwise unpredictable turns in both the market and their competitors. Real-life case histories are rarely so flattering, although a lot more interesting and instructive.

Whenever we have spoken to clients about what *really* happened in the early days of their businesses, we hear stories much more like Super Gran than Superman. Such stories don't feature the narrative of a great, all seeing hero or heroine. Instead, they tend to be characterised by early confusion and lack of knowledge, followed by either a dawning or sudden realisation of where an opportunity, market or even manufacturing technique might lie. Typically, however, it is not the first of these apparent 'epiphanies' that sets the course for success, and

---

7   Lannon J. and Baskin M. (eds) 2007. *A Master Class in Brand Planning: The Timeless Works of Stephen King*. Chichester: Wiley, p.51.

entrepreneurs often slog away for years before finally settling upon a winning formula. History is, of course, written by the victor.

Rory Sutherland sums up our tendency to create flattering histories and its consequences beautifully:

> *'You'll observe this phenomenon in most descriptions of battles, wherein victory is usually attributed (especially by the victors) to a few early strategic decisions made by the most senior people on the field. It simply doesn't do to say that Agincourt was the result of an unusually muddy field and some opportunistic Welshmen with big mallets.'*
>
> *'And it is an absolute must in an agency pitch, where the secret of success is to mug the audience with an irrefutable sequence of logic — even though every single person in the room knows that things will almost never turn out that way.'*
>
> *'... it matters to me as a creative person because, in maintaining the pretence that our business [advertising] works through a rational and sequential process, I feel we are perpetrating a minor fraud. And the victim of this fraud is creativity itself. Because in suggesting in our case studies that we arrived at success through process, we are falsely paying to logic a debt that we really owe to magic. The magic of imagination, or insight. And, as a result, we are causing the left brain to be overvalued at the expense of the right.'* [8]

True descriptions of the sequence of events in innovation are very rare. When did you last hear, 'We tried 95 things and were as surprised as everyone else when the last one worked'? It may be less flattering for those involved but such stories are undoubtedly more helpful for future generations of revolutionary innovators. They

8   Ibid p.43.

provide reassurance that even if the path is neither easy nor clear, it can still have a valuable destination; they make it obvious that eyes and ears should be kept open looking for more information, rather than firmly closed avoiding distractions.

One place to start is the list of market-changing inventions that were created more or less by mistake. For example, did you know that Skype was originally created as a peer-to-peer file sharing network before the application as a communication medium evolved? Or that Viagra, a drug now used to treat erectile dysfunction, began life as a treatment for high blood pressure and heart disease? It was only through trials of the drug during 1992, in the somewhat unlikely location of Merthyr Tydfil, that the medication's libido-enhancing power was realised after it was initially reported as an undesirable side-effect. Rogaine was also originally intended as a treatment for high blood pressure before its effects on hair growth were observed. WD40 was designed to prevent corrosion of nuclear missiles and was the fortieth attempt at a successful formula to do so, whereas Post-it notes were a by-product of a failed search for a strong adhesive. The list goes on.

3.4.1 The tale of David and Goliath

There's a reason why we don't tell children stories of the big guy crushing the little guys. Where's the fun, justice or inspiration in that? Instead, the stories that work are the ones where the little guy, against all the odds, manages to overcome adversity.

And it is presumably this preference for the story of the underdog which drives our bias towards the 'startup kills established player' story archetype. Whether it is true or not. As a result, examples of innovation which do not fit the romantic David and Goliath-type story are often forgotten or overlooked. People ask why Microsoft couldn't have invented Twitter, for example, discounting entirely that Microsoft did invent something similar and almost exactly as popular — Instant Messenger — several years previously.

But there is a bigger bias yet in this type of tale. As the story is told by the victor (and its triumphant PR team), it looks as if the single David of the startup — in a moment of self-assured mastery — fells the Goliath of the established business. But be sure that there was more than one potential David in this story. In fact, every Goliath is being attacked by a swarm of Davids, each with their own variation of the slingshot.

Put this way, it can be pretty tough on the big guy. With small but significant threats on all sides, the corporation must assess which is a real challenge to their business and which can safely be ignored.

Again a product of selection bias, when history comes to be written, the most dangerous opponents seem obvious. Of course, Kodak should have been most scared of the digital camera, and Microsoft of the tablet computer; but at the time that these threats emerged, the respective companies were already battling on multiple fronts that seemed, in terms of day-to-day business, much more important.

Without the benefit of hindsight, the selection of which battles to fight is a lot more difficult. The large player is likely to prioritise the markets in which they currently have the highest returns and margin even though these may not be the markets which eventually come to be the most lucrative or decisive. The market focus of the incumbent becomes a risk to the established player, although it is often only with the benefit of hindsight that the correct strategy can be identified.

We do not need to praise the David in the story for their choice of market space; the success of their selection is guaranteed by their status as eventual victor. A colleague of ours at Fluxx despairs when he hears the phrase 'What were the chances of that happening?', because he knows, the event having already happened, that the chances were exactly

100 per cent — and knowledge of this does not help us predict our own lives or companies' futures any better.

3.4.2 Magic: Lies, damn lies and retrospective business plans

One of the major challenges with attempting to copy the products and successes of competitors in your own market and other markets is that it can be extremely difficult to understand their financial plans and incentives, which are rarely public.

Speculation on how — or even if — companies are turning a profit is rife, with analysts and pundits queuing up to offer opinions on the potential business models of companies such as Dropbox and Twitter.

When startups spend a lot of time talking about their breakthrough financial models, it is worth remembering that their primary audience is likely to be the venture capitalist they would like to fund them, the bankers who already fund them, and the super-mega multinational they are hoping will one day buy them and get all these bankers and funders off their backs. Therefore, such statements may not be grounded in anything like reality. Conveniently, startups do not need to show their working (under the heading of proprietary information), and their maths may not need to work if their hype can blast them to the stratosphere of investment before their predictions need to come true.

As an example, we have spent considerable time analysing various 'freemium' models and find that many could never deliver profitable business under any circumstances. Have we missed something amazing, or is it possible there is simply nothing to miss? Beware the offhand interview and press release; just because it appears in the *Wall Street Journal*, doesn't mean it was subject to scrutiny or audit. If you can't make the sums work yourself, it is very unwise to assume that a model exists purely by the existence of other speculative businesses run on a similar basis — no matter how much venture capital is being poured into them. If you want to play this way, you should become a venture capitalist yourself.

Chapter 4

Innovation Today

S o if we strip back the hyperbole and distortion, what do we see of how large companies really approach the innovation problem? Exactly what is it that is really happening when large companies embark on revolutionary projects today?

What follows is a piecing together of our joint experiences at working with, or for, businesses both large and small in identifying, developing and launching products to market.

Yes, it's a bit of a litany of errors, any one of which would be enough to seriously derail anyone's confidence to nurture new business propositions. However, it is not our intention to gather together the worst, or even most amusing, war stories. Instead, we hope to represent fairly what is normal in business today with a depiction most will be able to readily identify with.

This shouldn't be about blame. The reason we've written this book, and indeed the reason we set up our company, is that we're hoping to find ways to avoid some of the mistakes we've observed (and made ourselves) in the past, and to find new (and more successful) ways of doing new things in the future.

Typically, these mistakes are not a result of employing incompetent people but rather they have been a product of good people stuck in impossible processes with badly mismatched expectations from those above them.

Of course, the mistakes we describe here often didn't appear obvious or silly at the time. For the most part, the teams we have been part of have been full of well-intentioned and bright individuals with good ideas and a well-thumbed management handbook. Neither would we interpret the actions of the senior executive teams described here as being Luddite, out of touch, only interested in short-term returns, and so on. Of course, the people who make up the boards of FTSE 500 companies are rarely any of these things, although they are very often under a great deal of pressure to deliver short-term results.

In our experience, senior executives have been — almost without exception — engaged, intelligent, thoughtful and deeply driven by the future success of the businesses they work for.

Ours is not a push for different people to be involved in the innovation process but rather for companies *to approach these projects differently.*

4.1 Where do ideas come from?

As we mentioned earlier, the ideas themselves are not the hard part. If you hold a workshop, you will come up with as many ideas as you have people. In fact, you'll probably have ten times as many ideas as participants.

This book certainly isn't about how to generate ideas.

Nevertheless, the actual source of an idea will typically impact significantly on the idea-development process itself. Ideas come with strings attached. Which strings will depend on where the idea came from. There tend to be three sources:

1. **Competitor.** The company may have been spurred on by the activities of a rival business or a similar company from a slightly different industry. In the case of a startup, the desire to improve on an existing product or a poorly-serviced market may be the key motivating factors.
2. **Executive.** Alternatively, you may have been directed to take an idea from a senior executive and develop it.
3. **An idea-harvesting process.** Finally, the company may have an ongoing programme of generating ideas and developing / investigating them.

4.1.1 Ideas from competitors and other companies

If the idea comes from a competitor (often disparagingly called the 'me too' idea), then it will come with a reasonable weight of expectation derived from the presumed success of the competitor. Since most companies favour publicising their successes rather than their travails and failures, information about the competitor's development process, commercial and user success is likely to be incomplete.

A good example of this is the trend for customisable home pages started by Google in 2005 and the BBC in 2007, following on from companies including Facebook and Pageflakes.

Clearly, it was not likely that these organisations would promote their new products in a lukewarm or negative way, suggesting that their products were in fact experimental and based on trends they had observed in other sites. Instead, both products were trumpeted as a revolution in the way web design should be implemented. And so many other large companies embarked on building on this presumed success. We'd regularly hear in design briefings that the Google and BBC examples should be followed in our own work. No further evidence would be given for this suggested approach.

The brands that followed this route, however, discovered that customers neither understood nor enjoyed customising their web experiences. The feature — like so many others — was rarely or never used, whilst having the unfortunate distinction of being extremely expensive to implement. Perhaps it was a feature which worked only for the super-brands of the web. Or perhaps it didn't work for anyone. Within a few years both BBC and Google had withdrawn the feature, with a lot less fanfare than accompanied its introduction.

There is also often a misconception that the competitor's success at innovation has created an entire category in which products can be launched and that if a new product can merely be created in time, it is guaranteed to be successful. Products such as Microsoft's Zune and Bing, Bebo, Google+ and others lead us to question the assumption that a large market size necessarily implies the room for multiple competitors. Another way to look at this is to question whether the competitor's product is really in the same market or solves the same customer problems, even if it has similar features.

In essence, the risk here is that the business will feel that its version of an idea or product need not be validated with the market. In addition, the business may struggle to develop the idea to create differentiation because it is so attached to the definition given to the product by the competitor. Did the Zune player need to have a circular method of interface control and a large colour screen? If Microsoft had instead decided it would make the smallest personal music player, could it have better stayed in the marketplace? Of course the answer is somewhere in the middle. Competitor-based ideas can certainly succeed. There are numerous examples (the Apple iPhone and then the Samsung Galaxy,

Friendster and then Facebook) of companies bringing products to market second or third and taking huge market share. But many of the 'common-sense' ideas about what can be learnt from competitors should be thoroughly questioned.

4.1.2 Executive

If, alternatively, senior executives advance an idea (even if the idea came from elsewhere) then there is a different sort of catch. They are unlikely to have recent hands-on experience with product development. Plus — owing to their position in the business — they may not be used to hearing the word 'no', or even 'perhaps'. This creates an issue for the team tasked with developing the product, and limits the scope they have for adjusting and advancing the idea.

Direct executive sponsorship of this sort can also lead to odd financial rules for the project at stake. Typically, it means that initial budgets are over-generous when a project starts but any extensions to that budget can be almost impossible to come by.

In terms of planning, we've often been surprised by how thin, yet confident in their predictions, early funding cases from senior executives can be. Empirical research has almost never been carried out. Financial modelling is often extremely simplistic and optimistic, if it is done at all. And yet these early funding cases typically come with promises attached of money that will be easily earned back in time.

By the time the brief arrives with the new product development (NPD) team there are two important but hidden constraints: the executives' spoken and unspoken expectation for the product (including what they have told other board members), and a financial promise which is built on the assumption that sufficient money has already been signed off to get the product to market. Even when NPD teams are firmly told that no such cost or revenue prediction exists, it will often lurk behind the scenes to be discovered later.

4.1.3 An innovation process

In many ways, the simplest starting point for a new product is when a team has been set up with an open remit of innovation. That's not to say it is easy being in one of these teams, or managing one. They come with their own unique challenges. New product development and innovation teams need to work extremely hard to maintain the respect of the rest of the business and avoid the stereotype of being seen as arrogant Post-it note-toting layabouts.

Typically, such innovation processes are either run in individual departments, perhaps with some central facilitation, or they are run by an R&D group, operating independently. As we'll see later, the nature of such teams, whether temporary or permanent, makes it almost impossible for them to be subject to 'management by results' or even 'management by exception'. This can make the teams seem simultaneously detached from the values of the business and unaccountable for their actions, which is not fertile ground for building trust and respect.

Innovation teams that do not have the support of the rest of the business will find that their ideas have a mysteriously short life and suffer a far higher rate of boardroom muggings and late-night murders than is usual.

There is also the risk that an innovation team will stray too far from the front line of the business they are in, and simply lose touch with the world that is moving ahead around them. An unnamed, but well-known, example exists amongst (at least one of) the UK terrestrial broadcasters. In order to compete in the context of rapidly-changing media markets, one such business set up its own innovation team. After many months locked in their top-floor innovation sanctum — replete with bean bags, table football and so on — the innovation team emerged with beards grown to tell the world about the bright shiny future they had envisaged, only to find that their vision had already become the somewhat faded past for many of their competitors.

And these risks go for any idea handed to them by anyone, anywhere in the business, whose concept then gets wrapped up in the politics and stereotypes surrounding the innovation team itself.

4.2 Money and politics

Another lesson from *The West Wing*. While Josh is trying to explain his role as Deputy Chief of Staff, he says: 'There are only two things that ever stop the government from doing anything: money and politics.' (Series 2, Episode 10: 'Noël'.)

The same may well be true in business. But the mechanism of how it works is subtly different.

4.2.1 Money

Let's look at money first.

At this stage we have the idea, with certain strings attached. We must decide how to develop it, how to move it forward. In the absence of any other options, many businesses will default to whatever process feels familiar for the allocation of resources.

Let's imagine that I am the manager of a company that produces chocolate biscuits in a factory. I become aware that I can improve output by streamlining the production process. A new biscuit-packing machine will allow me to cut the jobs of five staff and — in the process — improve both the number of biscuit packs that can be produced and the reliability of the entire operation.

In this sort of circumstance, I may allocate a small amount of budget to an initial feasibility study, ahead of a larger investment to actually install the machine and update processes so the machine will work. During this feasibility stage, I will also work out how long it will take for this combined investment to pay off. If the return on the investment is reasonable — two years, say — then I should proceed.

This approach, with little or no modification, is also commonly used for the development of new propositions. Perhaps not surprisingly, this is where the wheels start to fall off the wagon of large companies doing genuinely new things. Think about a typical scenario. In the first stage, a team will be assigned a small budget to generate ideas. A further budget is then granted to develop the ideas to a more complete proposal (with a business case) and then the team may be asked to report back monthly during the product's development.

At any stage, the management team may decide the project is not going according to plan and ask for changes or call the whole thing to a halt. Usually, however, the criteria for success or failure, at any given stage, are pretty unclear, leaving the project team to set their own criteria for continuation of the project.

In order of magnitude the first phase may be around a week, the second a month and the third from six months to a year. Anyone who has been involved in a genuinely new product development or 'revolutionary' development will see the challenge here instantly. Market knowledge and domain knowledge are both at their scarcest when the majority of the prediction is being carried out. Indeed, depending on the nature of the development, the market for which predictions are being made at this stage may not even be properly defined.

Particularly for more disruptive innovation, it's not just returns that are hard to predict. Costs are too. Faced with a total lack of clarity about what will be included in the project and even who will execute it, the project leader is incentivised at this early stage to maximise the budget they request to complete it. In order to secure the maximum amount of funding, the project leader will also, therefore, be forced to increase their predictions of likely return.

The mere act of identifying costs can also have a subtle reinforcing effect on the project leader's assumptions about the project. In order to get those costs, he or she will typically need to be able to brief internal and external parties on what the product itself will be. This has two effects. The first is to cement the detail of solution, at least in the mind of the project leader as he or she travels from meeting to meeting with an increasingly well-worn PowerPoint presentation. The internal or external development partner will be asked to both review the initial project assumptions and add their own input. Note also that in response to the prospect of lots of new potential work, they will always broadly say 'we think it's a great idea'. Both these factors add false validation to the plan; validation that is particularly unreliable given the intrinsic motivation of the development partner to want the project to go ahead, and to go ahead with the largest and least cautious scope possible.

We've had experience of this. When we've given honest feedback to potential clients that there are certain things that will have to be fleshed out or validated in order for their idea to succeed, we've consistently not been awarded the work, and are told that an alternative supplier or partner had 'more enthusiasm' for the idea or that they 'really got it' when we didn't.

So, the corporate process of validating investment strongly encourages teams to provide excessively positive forecasts for the product's success, and to fix important details of the product and proposition early, at the stage of the project where their understanding of the product is minimal. It puts them in a position where commitments to both delivery and return have been made for a project that barely exists. Perhaps most dangerously, it creates a negative and adversarial relationship between the executive and the team doing the product development before the project even starts.

Early-stage ideas are exciting to work on — at least in part because they are liberated from the weight of expectation. In judging ideas in this way, businesses virtually force their innovation teams into lying to them, inflating estimates of return, deflating estimates of costs and creating the illusion of certainty where little exists.

The product owner can tell themselves that they are doing the right thing for the business, essentially bypassing a dysfunctional system by making positive forecasts and projections. In their defence, it is so unreasonable to ask for forecasts at this stage that the project leader can scarcely be blamed for their excessive confidence in any numbers they do produce. Management, for their part, may tacitly understand that the projections are fiction; but know that they can chose to ignore this should it suit their purpose further down the line.

Faced with the sheer backwardness of the approval process, the manager of the innovation process is incentivised to trade bigger budgets for larger promises. Since they typically will have no idea what they're going to do (but don't want to admit this), bigger budgets give them the impression that they'll have the time and autonomy required to firm up the unknowns in private and make some tangible progress before having to report back. However, at the same time, the project leader is robbing themselves of the freedom to revise their plans, and to learn about the market or potential market from which they hope returns will come whilst committing to deliver something before they really understand the game. This will come back to haunt them.

By securing larger budgets early on, the manager now feels under intense pressure to produce results, whether that's a shippable product, positive feedback, customer orders, or actual financial returns. Their next move will, therefore, be an attempt to create a plan which can deliver results as early as possible.

Their priority shifts subtly from definition to doing. Essentially, the innovation leader is 'hoist by their own petard', a victim of their own design to escape scrutiny. In order to secure funding, the manager has been incentivised to conceal both the risk of the project and to gloss over its essential lack of definition or clarity. They have risen to the management taunt of 'don't you know what you are doing?' and agreed to play the game of intuitive prediction.

4.2.2 Politics

Politics is everywhere. But of course its impact can be incredibly subtle. The best professional politicians are those who can exert their influence invisibly when they need to and who can manipulate situations to their own advantage. Even in the glare of media scrutiny, the behaviour of Westminster and Washington politicians is complex and hard to understand.

Yet corporate politicians rarely face any scrutiny at all. Politics in this context is focused on the building of personal reputations and empires, gaining promotions, increasing pay and getting higher status inside and outside of the organisation, often at the expense of colleagues.

In these battles, the victor will be the one who can convince that their vision, focus and abilities are more likely to result in the successful delivery of a company strategy. Thus the successful corporate politician is adept at translating corporate strategy and the motivations of their audience to support their actions and intentions. All companies bear witness to many such competing or partially competing agendas, all dressed up in the language of corporate strategy.

Don't like it? Well, you're going to have to live with it. We've never found a company (or indeed club, society or political party) that is any different, because these behaviours are driven by very basic human motivations.

4.2.2.1 Jam tomorrow

A point strongly made by Clayton Christensen in his book *The Innovator's Dilemma*[9] is that established firms have a strong understanding of the dynamics of the market for existing products. They know the customers, they know the supply chain, and they know of the complex interplay between competitors and suppliers that make up any market ecosystem.

In addition, the different parts of their company's own ecosystem have a consistent bias in believing that the needs of these customers, suppliers, partners and distribution networks must be foremost to the exclusion of all else.

Innovative products therefore become, in Lewis Carroll's words, 'always jam tomorrow, never today', as they have to fight the status quo in order to be delivered.

Innovation might *always* be the right answer, but it is still trumped by *the customer is always right* which is always *always* right. In other words, today's business and today's customers quash the ability of an organisation to think seriously about new or emerging customers if their needs, market behaviours or economics are different to the here and now.

We've discussed the need for employees to be able to justify their behaviours clearly in terms of what is best for their employer. At no point do they believe that their employer will ever accept that today's customer was sacrificed to secure a more profitable future.

No matter how much energy is originally devoted to innovation, unless the executive is convinced that it can deliver jam today, it won't ever succeed.

---

9   Christensen, C. 1997. *The Innovator's Dilemma.* Cambridge, MA: Harvard Business School Press.

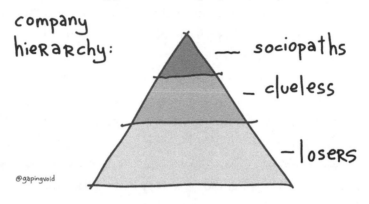

4.2.2.2 Sociopaths, clueless, losers

The legendary American cartoonist, Hugh MacLeod of Gaping Void fame (who was kind enough to design the cover for this book), famously sketched the following picture of company hierarchy.

These labels could be how each group would describe each other, perhaps they are merely the meanest interpretation of each group's faults, or they could simply be an example of Hugh's wicked humour and sense of perspective. The genius of the cartoon though, is that we instantly understand the idea and are then faced with the prospect of deciding which group we are in. The good news is that even if we can't make up our minds, we're really glad we're not in the other two!

Taking Hugh's extreme perspective, the top tier of the company is the most likely to suffer from (mild) sociopathic tendencies, has absolute faith in its convictions, is relentlessly determined to achieve their objectives and couldn't care less who gets in the way.

At the bottom of the pile are the losers, another extreme label to possibly describe those who *work to live* rather than *live to work*, but who are lambasted for this positive attitude and dismissed as wage slaves. For a while in America, this group might have been described as holding *McJobs*.

In the middle tier are the clueless, the somewhat hopeless salaried careerists, neither brutal enough for the top flight nor carefree enough for the bottom tier. This group of middle managers believes the dream they are sold by their sociopathic bosses and devote substantial energy to moving the business forward, even though they are in fact relatively inconsequential in the broad picture.

Our innovation managers, one has to assume, are drawn from the ranks of the clueless and the sociopaths, with the latter, sadly, more likely to succeed.

How true this picture really is of most businesses we leave to the reader, but it certainly hints at the complexity any of us faces when attempting to get existing businesses to do new things. The sociopaths will get on board (perhaps) if they can see how the move will benefit them. The clueless, often those in fact tasked with making the numbers work, resource allocation and so on, are likely to be more conservative and concerned about the immediate impact on their status or what their sociopathic leaders will do if they get it wrong. The losers will be concerned about any potential change to the status quo, seeing change and new 'opportunities' as euphemisms for disruption, risk and an increase in effort required.

In order to get our companies to do new things, we will need to think about how each of these groups — although we may use more politically correct and real-world descriptions of them — is (or is not) utilised to best effect and how their ability to derail the process because of personal agendas can be minimised.

4.3 Funding, politics and the alpha male

By the time we reach the development phase of the traditional process, the project leader will be fully embroiled in both money and politics, whether they like it or not.

In order to navigate the corporate approval process — which is put in place to prevent potential losses in shareholder value — they will likely have made a solemn promise about returns which is strongly predictive. They will also have embroiled themselves in politics, albeit unwittingly, and their financial promises are strongly linked to their status in the organisation.

Of course, no one could *reasonably* expect the individual to be able to deliver on these promises given the context of why and how they had to make them. But that boat has sailed: the process which got us to this point has been wildly inappropriate, inversely matching knowledge to the requirement to make promises.

Because of the bias of a typical project leader towards alpha behaviour — the defending of their position at all costs — they will often feel that they need to go along with the projections and early guesses they have been forced to make. However, as a consequence, from this stage onwards the appetite for finding out more is typically very low, in case it upsets the apple cart on which this project now finds itself. This is a shame, as this is precisely the time where learning is most likely to occur, and most beneficial.

Even at this relatively early stage, the project leader may have already set themselves on a course of no return, and they will continue to be required to pass formal and informal approval points which further narrow their options for change and learning. The leader is very likely to cherry-pick any evidence that points to the project being a success, of having a long-term market and likely high returns. Why? Because if the project continues to run, uncertainty in their own career will be reduced, as will the likelihood of previous reckless decision making being uncovered.

And what happens when doubts arise as to whether the project will be successful? From our own experience, on many occasions with very large financial investments, it's likely that new knowledge about a product or innovation's marketability, feasibility or viability will be dismissed. If it has come from outside the project team, it will be seen as politics; if from within, it will often simply be concealed to prevent the need to pass potentially bad news up the chain.

Again, we do not want to portray project leaders or their executives as frauds. They could each scarcely act any differently given the structures they are required to follow by their companies. This is why we will talk later about how to encourage new business leaders to behave more responsibly and, ultimately, more in their own interests, through creating a less adversarial, and more honest and open product development environment.

4.4 The heroic leader

We already touched on the personality types responsible for new product development in large companies — but, in a way, the skills possessed (or not) by these individuals, and their style of working, shouldn't surprise us. They are, after all, a product of corporate natural selection. Often, in order to be the sort of person who is chosen to lead a product development inside an enterprise you need to be:

- Someone who has been with the company a number of years and who has shown themselves to be a *safe pair of hands* in managing some aspect of the business
- Seen as a self-starter
- Perceived as confident and self-promoting

What we are describing here is an alpha personality. This will be someone who, in simple anthropological terms, is highly status-conscious and has achieved their status through either combative or deal-making behaviours.

Under pressure, such a leader is likely to feel that it is permissible to break rules in order to protect their pack (the team and initiative they are working on). Since the executive boards of most companies are made up of men and women with similar personalities, they will condone this rule-breaking as the best way to make things happen and perpetuate their own self-portraits of courageous or heroic leaders.

The risk here is that this sort of self-imagined heroism tends to ride roughshod over both the valued learnings of others as well as the rumblings of the political machine. But to be impervious to the views of others is to potentially miss out on important information that could make a radical difference to the product. Feedback that is viewed as being based on rivalry and jealousy could just as easily come from genuine customer intimacy and common sense.

The big heroic personalities of such leaders seem to encourage bigger risks to be taken, even when they are unnecessary. Board rooms are full of this sort of language: take big bets, double down, play your hand and so on. But when it comes to innovation, why do bets have to be big? Because they need to match the ego of the person taking them? If we can find a way to reduce the size of the bet, shouldn't we?

By removing emotional, political and financial attachment to ideas, we stand a greater chance of spotting the good ideas and their potentially great applications. It should go without saying that we need to work hard, be ambitious for our projects and conscientious in our approach, but those should not be excuses for the bloody-minded pursuit of projects whose very existence says more about their past than their future.

4.4.1 Leaving the pack

In accepting the job of working on new product development, the heroic leader may at first be under the impression that they have been promoted. This impression will soon change, however, when they realise they are destined to take on a much smaller team and carry out unfamiliar and uncertain tasks. In these circumstances, innovation will no longer feel like a fast-track to the top and, indeed, the more traditional routes via operations and finance will be almost enticing.

The tacit challenge for any such leader is the question of whether (and where) they will be allowed to rejoin the pack. If their project is a success, it may feel like the inception of a whole new business, with the heroic leader at the top. If the project fails, perhaps they will be allowed to take up normal duties once more. Or maybe they will need to find a new pack (project) either inside or outside the business, on which to focus.

Emphasising this separation, businesses often praise the *loner* qualities these leaders need to possess such as entrepreneurialism or the ability to be maverick. Leaders are encouraged to 'do what it takes', 'break all the rules' and so on to get the idea off the ground.

Of course, no one really wants these things. Were the project leader to genuinely start acting in a maverick manner with their superiors, they would be rapidly quashed.

How though, does it go down when these *loner* behaviours are exhibited with peers?

Here's really where the conceptual incentive for the heroic leader is a double-edged sword. At some stage in the development of the product in question (even if it is only the final stage when it must be test-marketed or researched), the innovator will need to seek support from their colleagues from the *normal* business. Now the leader's former colleagues feel much more like competitors (or even enemies) rather than supporters. Whilst they may not be overtly hostile to the new product, they could make it very hard for it to thrive in the real world. This will not be about challenging the product on rational grounds — how could it be when the product is in such early stages and typically lacks any firm test of its desirability? Rather, the business will begin to express negative sentiment because it feels the need to assert its expertise and experience — even though that experience is of *today's* market and company, not the one in which the new product will thrive.

Before you know it, the general consensus is that the product can't succeed. You will hear 'customers won't like it' or 'it will be hard to operate' before it has ever been introduced to a customer or anyone has made a concerted attempt to design the operational processes required to make it work.

How do businesses and new product leaders tend to respond to such premature negative sentiment? Far too often, these stresses result in the need to set more targets and constraints for the project. And now the heroic leader has fallen into the trap, attempting to defend a revolutionary project with the language and metrics used for reporting the progress of a normal project or other business-as-usual activity.

4.5 Jumping the gun

What is it that drives projects to get into the expensive building and delivery phase so early?

When we worked at a large technology firm some time ago, we would petition for a period of investigation and reflection before we started building the product in question. Typically, this phase would be known as discovery or definition, and in it we would seek to validate that we were doing the right thing, bring some shape to the idea so that customers could understand it, check whether the business case assumptions were reasonable, and try to answer some big questions about how the product might come to life and about the audience at which it was aimed.

We would regard two months of such work before development started in earnest to be a major victory, with clients sometimes wanting to reduce this time to just a couple of weeks or even days. The reason given for such expediency was typically the urgency of delivering the end product and quite often a cry of 'we've already done all that, just trust us'.

Of course, four to eight weeks is barely enough time to write down what the client *might* want and to create the most obvious of requirements for the project. And so it would be that we would commence extremely expensive projects with absolutely no evidence that the project was likely to be successful — but a really long list of what someone thinks should be in it based on little or no understanding of the customer, product or marketplace.

Just as surprising, we would often kick off projects of this sort knowing that the politics and approval process of the company we were working for would almost certainly doom the project to failure — either because the expectations already set were so out of sync with likely outcomes, or because the vested interests in the organisation would strangle the infant project before it could possibly prosper. Hardly the most fertile ground on which to succeed.

What was astounding in such projects was the way project-critical decisions are often taken with very little thought, or indeed barely taken at all, with innovation managers preferring to take default market choices rather than risk challenging established norms. Again, the thinking here seems to be that by following what others in market are doing, risk is reduced and, more specifically, the risk that the manager will be blamed for making bad choices is lower.

On one project, for example, a new charging model for a major consumer platform was being considered. The person responsible for the project eventually reverted to a charging model similar to that of a market leader after a senior executive suggested the new, and innovative, model was hard to understand.

The team was informed that the first proposed model was 'non-standard' and, therefore, too complex for a consumer to understand, thus proving too much of a risk. This was in a market where no other competitor had made the old model work.

After that, we would regularly be in a position where our entire design and development team thought the product they were developing was of questionable end-user value and would be unlikely to succeed. By necessity, our teams ended up believing in the client's confidence that the product would succeed in spite of this. However, that confidence was based on hubris alone, and the conviction that simply forging ahead would make it all work out in the end.

4.6 My CEO got an iPad for Christmas

Early predictions of failure — let's call it 'ambient negative sentiment' — can create obvious problems for a new product programme. We've also seen the risk at the other end of the spectrum, where programmes become overburdened early on by the weight of positive expectations.

In early 2011, we had numerous meetings at big companies that started with the onerous phrase: 'My CEO got an iPad for Christmas.' What they went on to say is that their CEO's expectations for all sorts of products and initiatives had now been reset by a casual conversation about how great it would be if their products were more like this.

And this has been a curse of innovation programmes for many years. A senior executive will look at work in progress and make an offhand comment: 'It would be great if it could do x' — or 'I imagine it's a bit like y', without ever having tested this suggestion, providing any evidence of its likely success, and without the innovation manager even agreeing to it. We suddenly have an expectation that will now proliferate across the entire business whenever that stakeholder discusses what the innovation team is up to.

Now the innovating team needs to build in the desired feature or behaviour into the product roadmap or enter a period of tedious politicking and negotiation to have the feature removed from the expectations of the executive. Without warning, the product goes from being a customer-centred solution to having a roadmap set by the wider business. Ideas don't need roadmaps until they're on the road. Once ideas are validated and proven and heading towards being a real product, that's when we consider the scope of the first release product, and how to structure the features that come after into a clear roadmap. However, many innovation leaders feel the need to anchor their programmes in the artefacts and planning that's used elsewhere in the operational business.

Often the team can set itself up for this problem by sharing internal documents without giving sufficient context. Vision visuals or early prototypes, for example, may feel like a great way to inspire the rest of the business and secure budget. However, the risk is that stakeholders can become excessively attached to a particular execution, feature or style, and then suddenly you have another target to meet, regardless of what you learn about the actual desirability of such a feature with real customers.

So be careful what you trade to build enthusiasm, or you could find your ambition to build a product customers want has been abandoned in favour of building a product which matches executives' expectations.

The phrase 'I would have expected...' is toxic to all innovation initiatives, especially speculative new business development. It is an outright symbol, if any is needed, that stakeholders have not been managed effectively and underlines a lack of understanding of how shaping and validation differs from execution.

4.7 Our heroic leader fails

In attempting to do the impossible, product owners have broken all the rules, twisted the truth and made many projections. Occasionally they will succeed. And if this happens, they will be perceived as superheroes, reinforcing the belief that maverick behaviour is the only way to achieve change in the organisation.

If they fail (which is statistically much more likely, as only one in ten new product development projects succeeds), the reasons for failure may never be well understood. Since so much has been invested, projects that fail often take many months or years to be successfully wound down. Their history is not written by the victors, since there are none. Instead various politically motivated accounts of failure will arise, and others will be discouraged from trying new things. Senior management, anxious to avoid further costly mistakes, may decide that greater (not different) governance is required for future projects.

Let's put all these process and cultural factors together:

- A framework for success which is inherently biased to today's business
- Staff who are looking to protect their positions by taking safe bets
- Resource allocation which may follow more traditional and conservative strategies than the owners of the business themselves intend
- Attempts to manage innovation projects based on predictability when these projects are inherently unpredictable
- The career trajectory of innovation managers being based on the outcomes of their projects

Given this, it should surprise us that innovation ever occurs in large firms at all.

If we were to go on to fill these pages with dozens of examples of how companies have failed to get their innovation programmes off the ground, the point of this diatribe wouldn't be to criticise or embarrass but, rather, it would be to marvel at the companies that have managed to overcome these processes and achieve breakthrough innovations in spite of them. It's these processes and conditions that make the innovation or new product area, potentially the most exciting part of any business, seem like way too much effort to bother with for the majority of staff.

4.8 Tough on innovation; tough on the causes of innovation

The upshot of the processes we've described above is that innovation can quickly become the poisoned chalice of a business. For all its initial appeal — 'It will be exciting', 'You will get to make your mark' and so on — it often quickly descends into an awkward trap where even the innovation team itself can seem uncertain about what value they are adding to the business, and can feel unable to explain this to the rest of the company.

All of a sudden this team feels like it is swimming upstream. It has inadvertently signed up to unachievable goals, become burdened by the expectations and assumptions of others, and senses the ever-looming deadline of the money running out. The team is no longer about coming up with something new that provides a long-term future for the business, but rather come up with something... anything... that will make money — and quickly. Even if this was not the intention of the initiative's sponsors and executive, it is an unavoidable outcome of the way the project is being managed. And products that make money (especially products that make money straight away) are much more likely to be closely related to the firm's current product line and based on an existing and well-proven business model of the company or its competitors. Not so much *innovation* as *renovation*.

And so, the business, by hook or by crook, appears to drive innovation from the breakthrough and potentially revolutionary outpost back into the 'normal' camp. What might have started out as interesting and market-changing ends up a compromise — a *me too* idea lacking differentiation, or a product extension of an existing line that is interesting, but won't be differentiating in the long term.

Now, perhaps, is a good time to look back at Kuhn. What is it that generates the right conditions for revolutionary science to outflank normal science?

In the world of science, it is a question of the evidence for change being overwhelming and a bright innovator suddenly being able to see things from an alternative perspective.

This would, indeed, be heartening in the corporate world. Bring on the visionaries! Do remember though; companies don't need to survive for an industry to continue. Revolutionary products can just as easily come from competitors — new or established — as from your company. Many of the best visionaries leave their companies because they are frustrated at their inability to innovate. Many of them go to innovate elsewhere, and often — sometimes many years later — come back to seriously challenge their former employers.

In the metaphor, the firms are the scientists, not the science itself — that's the market, or consumer area that they operate in. Failure to ride the revolutionary wave transforms a scientist to a footnote in the history books, rather than a leader in their field. Failure to ride a revolutionary wave in business has just the same effect, as so many firms have found.

As Clayton Christensen argues in *The Innovator's Dilemma*: 'Because an organisation's structure and how its groups work together may have been established to facilitate the design of its dominant product, the direction of causality may ultimately reverse itself: The organisation's structure and the way its groups learn to work together can then affect the way it can and cannot design new products.

The reason is that good management itself was the root cause. Managers played the game the way it was supposed to be played. The very decision-making and resource allocation processes that are key to the success of established companies are the very processes that reject disruptive technologies: listening carefully to customers; tracking competitors' actions carefully; and investing resources to design and build higher-performance, higher-quality products that will yield a greater profit. These are the reasons why great firms stumbled or failed when confronted with disruptive technological change.'[10]

Successful companies *want* their resources to be focused on activities that address customers' needs, that promise higher profits, that are technologically feasible and that help them play in substantial markets. Yet, to expect the processes that accomplish these things to *also* nurture disruptive technologies — to focus resources on proposals that customers would reject today, that today offer lower profit, that underperform existing technologies and can only be sold in insignificant scale — is akin to flapping one's arms with homemade wings strapped to them in an attempt to fly. You just won't get the idea off the ground.

4.9 A new entrant does the 'impossible'

The end to this story, when things do go wrong, is that a new firm will enter the market and do what feels impossible to the (now embattled) new product development team working in the same area at the existing business.

However, let's not blame them for this thinking, because there are at least five things working dramatically in favour of the new entrant:

- They do not have to support the cost structures of the existing business.
- They are not pre-programmed to think in terms of one commercial model. They are prepared to invest time and effort in a project that may make relatively low returns as they may well translate into higher overall returns in the longer term.

---

10 Christensen, C. 1997. *The Innovator's Dilemma.* Cambridge, MA: Harvard Business School Press, p.31.

- Very often, the new firm will be set up based on the strong belief in the innovation in question. Often the staff of the new firm is made up of former employees of the old business who felt their ideas could never come to fruition in that environment.

- New companies have no customers by whom they can be led astray. Customer focus is the defining feature of many of the world's most successful businesses but it is not always the best way to come up with something new.

- Finally — but most importantly — numbers. It may feel like a startup is a lone force fighting against an established business, but in fact it is part of an army. Any established company has a practically infinite range of competitors. And it is history that will judge which of these competitors is strongest. Again, this is an example of selection bias, as we described it earlier, with the incumbent Goliath slain by not one David but an army of Davids, each with their own bizarre version of a slingshot.

And what does the post-match analysis at the big company reveal? Why do the Goliaths believe they were so easily beaten? The politically minded will make sure that they use the failure to their own personal benefit. The accountants may push for more strenuous approval processes for new products. Still others may suggest more innovation is required.

It is unlikely we will hear senior managers suggest that they were unable to manage the process successfully; neither will the alpha project leaders declare that they were too self-assured or that their magic powers of prediction were not up to the game.

Chapter 5

Driving Forces

But what are the underlying factors at work in companies that drive the actions we've explored so far?

The behaviours we'll talk about in this chapter are so commonplace that they must — at least partly — be as much built into ourselves as human beings, as into the businesses in which we work. Is there some hardwiring in our brains that means we are predetermined to act in this way? And what forces are at work outside of our own selves that mean we are prevented from doing new things? Let's break down the forces that compel these ways of acting.

5.1 Inappropriate management techniques

Traditional management focuses on generating repeatable outcomes and ever-increasing efficiency from capital. This obviously isn't how most managers would describe their jobs but it is the reality about how most businesses operate. As Eric Reis points out in *The Lean Startup*, this method of organising and operating businesses has been extremely successful, and has allowed organisations to consistently improve profits while reducing headcounts across virtually all industries.

In order to keep the machine running smoothly, managers are incentivised directly based on the returns they can generate (management by results) and focus their actions on resolving issues with underperformance (management by exception). Predictability, therefore, is vital. Experienced managers have learnt that they can improve the performance of their teams with a variety of management techniques, including *softer* management fads such as neuro-linguistic programming (NLP) or developing a better understanding and consideration of emotional intelligence, but at the core remains a strong emphasis on the setting and measuring of targets. Where targets are met, the managers and their workforce should be rewarded. When targets are missed, souls must be searched, Christmas parties postponed and the spectre of the redundancy scythe may even be invoked. The message is clear. We'll either have more performance or less cost. And you don't want to know what 'less cost' really means.

This process has been refined over many years, helping us to understand which incentives are most effective, how teams can be structured and how staff should interact. Companies have toyed with many models for incentives and rewards at different levels of the hierarchy. Personal goals are aligned with corporate goals, values are aligned to effectiveness, and so on.

More progressive businesses may have found ways to soften the experience of working in a performance-led management environment, creating a more social contract with employees by allowing for flexible working practices and extending benefits beyond straight-forward financial remuneration. But it is in adversity that we understand the true character of these working relationships. And it is in lean times that most corporates revert to form.

The obvious challenge for companies doing new things is that innovation and new product teams can rarely (if ever) be managed using the same techniques that work so well for running the day-to-day business.

When we set out to create new products, the process will have several phases — none of which should really come as a great surprise but, equally, none of which fits into a traditional management philosophy.

We'll discuss the process in more detail later on but for the time being assume it follows these four basic stages:

1. **Learning and context-setting.** Even the largest and most long-established companies can benefit from taking a step back from day-to-day operations to understand who the main players in the market are, how innovation might disrupt that market, and how the current products are performing. Typically, companies need to look outside their business for these insights. Ideally, the team that will take on the responsibility for developing new products will have this knowledge and continue to top up that knowledge throughout the project.

2. **Idea creation.** Having understood the context, and learned from other businesses and industries, the first stage in creating a new product, proposition or service is to generate a long list of prospective ideas. This is an area that many companies feel more comfortable with — the brainstorm and its ilk having long-since invaded most corporate environments.

3. **Testing and developing ideas.** A single idea can take many forms. This stage is about working out exactly what sort of proposition you will develop from that idea in the context of your company and your customer. When you've done that,

you need to prove that your assumptions are correcting by validating in the real world that customers will accept and want your proposition and that you have the necessary resources and wherewithal to build and operate it.

Stage three is an area which fits particularly poorly with standard management practice. In fact, all too often, it is simply not done at all. Perhaps the urge to skip this step is because no one wants to have their name attached to a failure.

It is still tough to separate the concept of a negative project outcome from a negative commercial (and, therefore, personal) outcome. So, while the subsequent design phase is made up of higgledy-piggledy complexity and risk, many will find the familiarity of it more comfortable than the uncertainty of discovering the truth in the ideas, and making tough decisions on what you should *really* be doing.

Yet, this phase is the keystone of the way we believe products should be developed, and we have considerable evidence to show that as a process, it is a critical element to doing innovation well.

To do it requires that corporate leaders must trade in their gut instincts and judgement based on many years of experience for an evidence-based process of validating that products are viable, feasible and desirable to customers.

When companies do start testing their ideas in this way, they will certainly find that a new approach to management is required. If we're going to spend four weeks, or even four days, on running a test to learn what will make for a good product, we need to assume that it is at least as likely that the test will result in *failure* as that it will result in *success*. We try to ignore both these words and instead focus what every test always generates; learning — and how this is the most valuable commodity.

Some simple analysis of innovation programmes, in fact, tells us that any individual product is much more likely to fail as to succeed, and for every successful product there are hundreds, or thousands, that *failed*. For all of our best intentions, planning and experience, we will be wrong at least as often as we are right in our ability to predict outcomes.

This is hardly the language of corporate business. Imagine if you asked one of your team to predict whether a new software release would go well and they said: 'Possibly, we'll see what happens.' Imagine you asked the manager of your production line whether she expected to produce the same quantities as last month and she replied: 'I think so. But then again it might be only half as much.' Emergency meetings would be required; HR would need to be involved. Performance would need to be managed back *'on track'*. If shareholders found out, your CEO would be up against the wall.

So here's the tricky bit. First, you have to accept that you will always achieve a better end result by testing and learning; that the best instincts of your trusted leaders are simply not reliable enough.

And secondly, once you have made that call, once people have become convinced that products should be the result of methodical experimentation, you must manage the teams and cycles of that work proactively with a keen eye on what is being learned and arm the team with the tools, techniques and motivations that will lead to the right outcomes — better products that customers will love.

An important part of the answer at this stage is to reduce the risk as far as possible. As the writer and consultant Euan Semple argues, the smaller the 'I', the less you need to care about ROI (return on investment). Doing low cost experiments reduces the sting when you need to back up and try something different.

4. **Turning good product ideas into good products.** If stage three is about identifying a product that can be built (feasible), will be bought (desirable) and can be sold and operated (viable), then stage four is about carrying out the millions of detailed

tasks required to make that product as good as it can be. This is the flawless execution of that idea you now know to be solid.

Here too, businesses can often adopt very dysfunctional behaviours. This is especially true when companies have decided to skip over stage three entirely. That is to say, that ideas have arrived almost complete as designed solutions, and the implementation of that idea — even though there is no evidence that anyone actually wants it, nor that it's viable or feasible — is seen as the final stage of getting it to market.

Between 2007 and 2009, HMV invested several million pounds into the development of a social network, having declared this intent to the London Stock Exchange (setting stakeholder expectations, of course). Aside from executive hubris, and the fact that MySpace was doing well in the area of youth music, there was no evidence that such a social network would be valued or used by its audience, or that HMV had any ability to make this work. After almost a year of development and a year of operation, the 'Get Closer' project was eventually shut down in September 2009. The challenge was that before the HMV project was even started, the executive team had decided on an execution that they simply believed would be successful based on gut feel and confidence in the HMV brand.

But once we're in this final stage, we may find that traditional management practice can be just as debilitating.

Development of a product is extremely complex. Almost always you will need to combine business design, customer-facing design or service design and technical design. You will then need to integrate multiple work streams, make sure that you're regularly reviewing progress with stakeholders and customers, and attempt to maintain quality throughout the operation, despite delays and challenges from many sources.

Again, the process tends to be strongly steered towards the predictive end of the spectrum. Managers are often visibly relieved after the uncertainty of the previous phases that the project is now seemingly on certain ground — even if those learning phases have been dramatically curtailed. This is the part of the project where we can construct plans and, if we miss our targets, we should be able to get answers as to why they've been missed. Once again we see that managers prefer better understood processes, even where they are not helpful or appropriate.

In *The Lean Startup*, Eric Reis makes a very good point about the ability to predict your development progress: if you're building a product that no one wants, it doesn't really matter if you are on schedule or within budget. And yet the psychology here seems relatively simple to understand. Faced with the huge uncertainty which is intrinsic in any new product development, it is natural to try and focus on those things which are easier to grasp. When surrounded by things which can't be managed, it's very tempting to focus on other things that can be — a bit like rearranging the deck chairs on the Titanic.

And, if anything, learning is even less popular during this phase than in previous ones.

The challenge is that we are just as likely, or more likely, to learn about the product, its market and technology during this phase than before. This is not a negative reflection on the proposition development process. It is a reality about the inability of the human brain to predict what people will want, or to know in advance how the development process will turn out.

But more to the point, new information gained during development should clearly not be seen as a threat to a deadline. Such thinking is a very project management-heavy view of the world. The product matters most, and if we find out information during the process which makes the product better, this can only be a good thing.

5.2 Being responsible and
spending other people's money

American humourist and commentator P.J. O'Rourke (borrowing heavily from Milton Friedman) provides a very simple description of the challenge of motivating teams within companies. He describes four ways to spend money:

1. You spend your money on yourself. You're motivated to get the thing you want most at the best price. This is the way middle-aged men haggle with Porsche dealers.
2. You spend your money on other people. You still want a bargain, but you're less interested in pleasing the recipient of your largesse. This is why children get underwear at Christmas.
3. You spend other people's money on yourself. You get what you want and price no longer matters. The second wives who ride around with the middle-aged men in the Porsches do this kind of spending at Neiman Marcus.
4. You spend other people's money on other people. And in this case, who gives a sh*t?'[11]

O'Rourke goes on: 'Most government spending falls into category four. Which is why the government keeps buying us Hoover Dams, B-1 Bombers, raids on Waco cults, and 1972 Federal Water Pollution Control Acts.'

The same logic can apply to unencumbered innovation or product development teams. Would they proceed in quite the same way if they were spending their own money? Would they react to evidence of flaws in their hypotheses differently?

---

11   O'Rourke, P.J. 1994. *All the Trouble In The World, The Lighter Side of Famine, Pestilence, Destruction and Death.* New York, NY: Atlantic Monthly Press (p.200).

5.3 Human factors

A theme which has emerged frequently in the social media era is why attempts to make Facebook-style communities come to life inside organisations seem doomed to failure. For employers, the appeal of this idea is great. Imagine if staff self-organised online to seek out similarly-minded colleagues. Imagine if they uploaded details of what they were up to so that others could serendipitously stumble across it and help them. Imagine if we could have our cleverest and most ambitious people constantly trying to improve on each other's work — a kind of semi-public competition to get the best out of each other.

It could be a revolution on the same scale that Facebook has been outside of work.

And there are examples too — early social networks were formed inside companies like Xerox to share information about how to repair devices. Small-scale examples abound of groups using the new technology in new and interesting ways.

The challenge we have seen, though, to transforming these early buds of success to new ways of working are that the behaviours and motivations of those sat behind desks are not necessarily rational, and they are certainly not social in the straight-forward sense.

In *Predictably Irrational*[12], Dan Ariely draws a sharp distinction between the social norms that govern our daily lives and interactions and the market norms which govern our working life. Various experiments show that as soon as we switch from social norms to market norms, we will become much more insular, self-reliant and much more cautious about what we should and shouldn't be doing.

There is a reason why those of us who have been in work for a while find it much easier to understand negative or counterproductive work

---

12 Ariely, D. 2008. *Predictably Irrational: The Hidden Forces that Shape Our Decisions*. Scarborough, Ontario: HarperCollins, Canada.

behaviour, such as working slowly or being obstructive. It's because we have ceased to expect social norms to apply in our office environments, even when outside the office colleagues have a social relationship in which those norms *do* apply. Have you ever worked with a colleague who is recalcitrant and unhelpful in the office but chatty and supportive off-campus?

The reasons for this should be obvious but can often be obscured by the pretence of a supportive social community.

1. **People want to keep their jobs.** Even if people don't like their current jobs, they'd rather keep them than lose them. That is, people would like to retain total control over their role in the business, and whilst they'll resign if and when they're ready, they don't want to be fired. In order to do this, people feel they need to be performing, i.e. doing their job not necessarily well, but better than the average performance in the company.

2. **People would like to earn more, work fewer days a year, have more control over their own schedule and have fewer people telling them what to do**. There's a much longer list than this but these are basically the soft factors that come with being an employee enjoying longer standing and greater respect. There is also a perception (albeit a perverse one) that being further up the corporate ladder increases job security, presumably because it decreases the number of peer-group competitors as the pyramid at the top of most firms gets narrower.

3. **Status is important in companies**. Status comes from being regarded as influential and important within the business. The old-fashioned key to the executive washroom is a brilliant example; there's little actual benefit but it is a strong and visible signifier of making progress inside an organisation.

So, unlike in social situations, the workplace sees very active competition for various commodities: job security, status, salaries. The most successful operators are those who can gain these commodities without being seen to be fighting too ruthlessly to achieve them. Or to give it its proper name: companies suffer incredible *politics*.

These three simple starting points explain some very influential and important drivers in business:

5.3.1 Ownership bias — The toothbrush effect and 'not invented here'

This is the theory that opinions and ideas are likely to be much more valuable to the person who came up with them in the first place. Another name given to this theory is *the toothbrush effect* on the basis that everyone needs a toothbrush but nobody wants to use anyone else's. Similarly, we have all witnessed brainstorms where the more alpha the participant, the more territorial they are about their ideas, slogging it out with all-comers to make sure their brainwave is selected and adopted. And, of course, what everyone who receives that idea later might well experience is what an innovation team might call the *not invented here* bias.

The thought process here is hardly complex to understand. Anyone who's had an idea praised by others will know the feeling of pride that comes directly from that. In a work context, where the adoption of a person's idea could lead to a change in the business, then status, security and return are all on the table too.

Although no one wants to be caught putting an idea forward purely because they were the idea's parent, it is remarkably common to see this happening, and common too to see people desperately trying to cover up their attempts to further their own ideas.

As described in *Predictably Irrational*, the effect can be used to drive positive as well as negative behaviour. Ariely describes an experiment whereby one set of participants was asked to *create* a solution to a problem based on a collection of jumbled up words. A second set was asked to *adopt* an already-completed solution. In fact, the jumbled up words were simply the complete solution the second group received, but in a different order. Invariably, the first group would put the words together to form the same solution as the other group. However, the first group's attachment to the answer was much stronger — participants would do much more to see it enacted and to protect it from being adapted or varied in anyway. Even the minor act of putting the words together in the right order was enough to create an attachment to a finished idea.

Without exaggeration, we would say it is this particular human trait that can be most toxic in an innovation team if not correctly identified and harnessed.

5.3.2 Opportunity cost

In work situations, if some effort or project does not benefit the employee in some way, it can feel as if it has a negative effect. This is partly real and partly imaginary. Doing something for someone else that has no personal benefit but which may be a good long-term political play may distract time and effort from the potential of things that would otherwise benefit us now. This is what economists term *opportunity cost*.

What if the alternative to doing something that has no personal benefit is actually to do nothing? In this situation the opportunity cost doesn't really exist, but then a more primitive driver kicks in, which is to preserve energy and enthusiasm for the next fight, the next project, the next opportunity to benefit. Unless an employee will get caught out and be seen to be engaging in this behaviour, and reprimanded for it, why *wouldn't* they go down this route? It would certainly explain much of the apathy that the innovator faces from the rest of the business when trying to move a breakthrough idea forward.

5.3.3 Zero sum

A more divisive, if less common, counterproductive behaviour is actively working *against* a colleague. Clearly, this is worse than doing nothing: it is actively sabotaging the projects of another. Those new to the workplace can find this sort of behaviour truly shocking. Indeed, it can take a while before recruits are able to recognise such behaviour for what it is, because it seems so counter-intuitive, and that is because it is so unlike the norms that exist outside of business. But in fact it can be quite rational. As we've said, the supply of status, benefits and job security is fixed and by reducing the number effectively able to compete for it, our anti-hero effectively improves their chances of a better allocation.

The behaviour is strictly based on a zero sum (you win, I lose) view of the business world.

5.3.4 Perverse estimation and procrastination

When managers ask staff (or indeed, suppliers and partners) to estimate a task, they will insist that the number provided is merely to help forecasting and you will not be held to it. In fact, the suggestion of approximation is there purely to encourage the employee not to hedge, i.e. to inflate the estimate in fear of underestimating it. As soon as the project starts, all estimates will be expected to be solid. Employees will be praised for spending less time than predicted and eyed wearily and with suspicion for doing the opposite. The employee quickly learns to over-egg their estimates. With nothing to lose and everything to gain from mis-estimation, project plans can quickly become vastly bloated and distorted. Optimism vanishes entirely.

Of course, once again, no one wants to be caught doing this, so pessimism is dressed as prudence. This is a very fine line to tread. At what stage does the employee run the risk of looking slow and unproductive? A great deal of delicacy is required.

Once estimates have been received, just how motivated is the employee really to do better than promised? Not very. They should be on time or a little early, but being way too early runs the risk of making estimation seem poor, squeezing future ability to bloat estimates and more to the point, perhaps hastens the next estimation round, which few look forward to. Thus, work behaves similarly to how Boyle's Law dictates the behaviour of gas: it expands to fill the space (time) available.

5.3.5 Innovation is popular, so long as nothing has to change

As noted above, we've never found anyone who is against innovation per se. In words, if not deeds, innovation is extremely popular.

Why, then, do employees oppose innovation in their actions, if not in their words? Here we find the conflict between the realities of work motivation and the powerful motivator of self-image.

When discussing the future, most employees have the nous to understand that the bosses will want optimism. And so, most employees want to present themselves as (and indeed believe themselves to be) dynamic, flexible and unafraid of change. Whether it is true or not is another matter. We know from experience that when placed under a little pressure, most people will fall back to the things they are most comfortable with. Many really aren't built for innovative work, and particularly for revolutionary projects. They simply find the requisite level of uncertainty too unsettling. Consequently, behaviours tend to bear out what is subconsciously desired; stability and certainty.

5.3.6 Misallocation of resources

In *The Innovator's Dilemma*, Clayton Christensen makes a very insightful observation about resource allocation in large companies. No matter what the Chief Executive writes in the annual report, or what the head of each important team says at a conference about the business priorities, it will be a middle manager who in fact makes the resource allocation that decides what the company cares about. Many companies enjoy a military analogy: target markets, aggressive campaigns, guerrilla tactics, and so on. Well, in this analogy, the platoon lieutenant out in the field is setting his own agenda and may in fact be pointing the troops in a totally different direction from the commander's intent.

Whilst cheerfully acknowledging the company's supposed direction, such middle managers can reallocate resources towards their own perceived priorities with plenty of air cover (in this case, plausible excuses) based on customer priorities, and so on.

Peculiar they may be, but these corporate behaviours are amongst the least base we have seen. In fact, the middle manager — described as 'clueless' in Hugh's earlier cartoon — may well be making choices they strongly believe are correct for the company and its customers — and in fact, given the day-to-day pressures, seem very prudent and hard to argue with.

More dastardly drivers exist too of course: outright personal rivalry, jealousy, individual vendettas — and worse — form the lower level of non-rational behavioural drivers. Almost all of these types of actions would result in an individual being viewed dimly in a social context. In a work environment, they will be praised and rewarded, especially once they've been dressed up in the name of the best interests of the company or its customers.

Economists describe these behaviours as 'moral hazard' or the 'principle-agent problem'. By acting in a short-sighted way in order to maintain their status, employees may have a negative impact on the long-term future of the business, but not one which will impact upon them directly. They are, then, in a position to decide consciously or not whether their chances are better doing the right thing for long term company success, but putting themselves at risk, or doing the wrong thing whilst improving their personal lot. Are they more likely to lose their job through being perceived as poor performers, or through the long-term failure of their business to innovate?

5.4 The structures we build into businesses

this is great! i just need to run it by bob and cheryl and ken and pam and steve and henry and mary and ben and anna and rajish and melinda and chris and caroline and ted and alan and shannon and lexie and jim and valerie and thomas and vincent and pauline and shel and gus and karrie and miles and fiona and sheila and tony and bill and richard and connie and karen and charles and paulie and james and michael and sarah and joseph and lisa and don and george and jeff and kimberly and jason and michelle and marcus and andrew and laura and sophie and joshua and daniel and ethan and lucy and alex and liam and max and amy and hannah and katie and adam and muhammed and jasmine and " " "

"the endless organizational consensus"

Are the structures under which your company operates conducive to new projects in general? How have they supported recent new projects in particular?

The creation of a well-oiled interdependent set of departments in a business is one of the ways in which companies create effective competitive advantage. In order to achieve this, the teams must be able to operate independently. Each team will have its own hierarchy, its own ways of working, and so on. And like all organisations, each department will defend itself against perceived attack. No manager wants to get involved with the unexciting HR euphemisms of downsizing and rationalisation. Equally, any change which threatens a department will be met with subtle and not so subtle responses, a sort of union of individual interests.

We have seen this many times. Promising new ideas will be dismissed because they require other departments to cooperate in delivery, or ideas will be passed around different departments for input until they return barely recognisable. Ever more layers of poorly-considered ideas will be piled on like a Christmas tree overloaded with decorations until it is ready to collapse.

Where a new idea threatens an existing team it may be deliberately amended beyond recognition or pointlessly delayed by calls for further research or study. The larger that team, or the more significant its role in the day-to-day economics of the company, the more those defensive measures will seek not only to kill the new idea, but to silence all talk about it.

'Organisations are sticky, they struggle to escape the past. Even if you properly divide the labour, it is easy to build a Dedicated Team that acts like a Little Performance Engine (a mirror of the normal business)... .'[13]

In a 2008 talk at the Yale School of Management, Gary T. DiCamillo, a former Chief Executive at Polaroid, said one reason that the company went out of business was that the revenue it was reaping from film sales acted like a blockade to any experimentation with new business models.

'We knew we needed to change the fan belt, but we couldn't stop the engine,' he said. 'And the reason we couldn't stop the engine was that instant film was the core of the financial model of this company. It drove all the economics.'

---

13   Govindarajan, V. and Trimble, C. 2010. *The Other Side of Innovation: Solving the Execution Challenge.* Cambridge, MA: Harvard Business School Press, p.52.

Looking at Polaroid's competitors, how else do we explain Kodak's 1996 decision to build, at a cost of around $12bn, a hybrid film and digital camera; the *Kodak Advantix Preview*, a film camera that allowed images to be previewed? Would the thought that film should be part of the product have even been considered in a business that didn't have a huge team who had spent years doing nothing but producing and refining film products?

The Kodak engineer who made the invention of the first digital camera is quoted by the *New York Times* as describing the management reaction, 'That's cute — but don't tell anyone about it'[14] because of the threat it posed to the core film business.

In Tracy Kidder's *The Soul of a New Machine*,[15] he recounts how one long-term Data General engineer, Tom West, was given the chance of a hands-on look at the VAX, the new computer from his fiercest competitor, DEC: 'Looking into the VAX, West had imagined he saw a diagram of DEC's corporate organisation.' The engineer was reassured because the way in which the VAX was designed reflected everything that was wrong with the DEC organisation itself; it was complex, overburdened with unnecessary protocols between different functional elements, and inherently 'cautious'. DEC's own product had now become just like the badly communicating, dysfunctional set of competing departments that had worked to design and build it.

5.5 Thinking of marketing as an add-on

Every company has a centre of balance. Sometimes this is in the marketing team — but rarely. More often production, operations and accounts hold sway. I was a member of the Marketing Society for many years and could rely on the debate about why marketing wasn't sufficiently represented in the boardroom to surface quarterly in the

---

14   http://www.nytimes.com/2008/05/02/technology/02kodak.html?pagewanted=all
15   Kidder, T. 1982. *The Soul of a New Machine*. New York: Avon Books, p.32.

Society's otherwise excellent publication *Market Leader*. Perhaps one of the reasons that marketing is sometimes not taken seriously enough is that marketers persist in constantly having this discussion. The other is that marketing teams are better known for execution than strategy, and some marketers lack the ability to correctly position their profession in the context of new product development.

In any case, it is not uncommon for organisations to suggest that their marketing teams get involved in product development only after the project has been more or less completed. Like a kind of glorified packaging team, the marketers are handed a fully-fledged product and asked how they would make it popular.

This is a very effective way to reduce the classic 'Four Ps of marketing' — price, product, promotion and place — down to just the one: promotion.

Marketers will often have a strong idea of current market dynamics, who the potential customers are, and where their needs may lie. This perfectly positions them to make expert contributions to the design and definition of product characteristics, distribution and pricing.

In addition, what is learned about the product and its potential audience during the proposition and development phases will be invaluable in launching and marketing the product further down the line. You can't test a product without testing its marketing. The way the product is positioned and explained is just as much part of a product as its design and build.

At Time Inc., where Fluxx helps run a new product development lab, no product passes muster on the business case unless someone can outline in marketing terms how it is going to find a large enough audience to make it work commercially.

Chapter 6

What Makes
Products Successful?

A s you go through the process of learning more about your product, its market and its manufacture, you should get an ever-clearer idea of how likely it is to do well, and there will be a number of factors emerging that will strongly correlate to its success or failure.

These factors have been well understood for many years. It is not a comprehension of the facets of a success which is lacking but, more often, the willingness of businesses to research these factors, and — more to the point — a willingness to respond to the answers they find when they ask the questions.

Studies of why products fail report the same findings over and over again, and have done for decades. There is simply no mystery to this at all. The mystery, instead, is why those involved in innovative product development seem insistent on re-learning these lessons on every outing.

The four reasons products fail are these:

1. Poor alignment with the market — in other words, customers don't want it.
2. Technical issues — in other words, it is difficult and/or expensive to build.
3. Insufficient marketing effort — in other words, its benefits haven't been communicated compellingly to the relevant audience.
4. Bad timing — in other words, the product took too long to get to market and/or was beaten by a competitor.

This is not armchair punditry; these are the answers given by the unlucky owners of unsuccessful or never-launched products as to what went wrong. They are as easy to understand as they are unsurprising. And they feed directly into the observations about what will make new products successful.

In *New Products, Key Factors in Success* (1990)[16] Robert Cooper and Elko Kleinschmidt (inventors of the now widely used Stage-Gate product development methodology) analysed over 200 product launches, and list the key factors they find to correlate statistically with product success. Although refined through numerous future studies by Cooper and others, opinion on success factors remains broadly the same today. Again, none of these will make you jump out of your chair in surprise:

---

16   Cooper, R. and Kleinschmidt, E. 1990. *New Products, Key Factors in Success.* Stage-Gate International.

1. A superior product that delivers benefit to its users

Products which deliver real and unique benefits to customers are far more likely to succeed in the marketplace. Perhaps at first this seems glaringly obvious. It should actually come as a relief. Quality and differentiation are indeed vital, in fact they are the single biggest determinant of success — products in the top 20 per cent by this criterion have a success rate of 98 per cent. Those in the bottom 20 per cent have a success rate of just 18.4 per cent.

How is this judged? The criteria are relatively simple:

- Does the product offer unique features not available on competitive products?
- Does the product meet customer needs better than competitive products?
- Does the product have a higher relative product quality?
- Does the product solve a problem the customer had with a competitive product?
- Does the product reduce the customer's total costs (creating value)?
- Is the product the first of its kind in the market?

The implication should be simple (albeit not easily done): learn about the customer, understand and empathise with their world, be creative in solutions, use a customer feedback cycle to refine ideas and make something people want.

2. Planning before developing

How thoroughly and clearly have you understood the product before we begin development? As noted above, we've seen companies leap straight to development before a proper understanding of the product has been created. By deferring execution in favour of better definition (of the market, technical and business characteristics of the product) we significantly increase the odds of success. Although Cooper emphasises that this definition 'must be based on solid evidence, not speculation' (p.12):

'In too many projects, we witnessed a product idea that moved directly into development with very little in the way of homework to define the product and justify the project. More often than not the results were negative.' (p.16)

Even Cooper's choice of word, 'homework' is interesting in this context. Why homework? Presumably more because it is work that people avoid or put off, rather than something which people need to do individually or at home.

All too often this work is indeed seen as an optional luxury which gets in the way of the real work. Yet, failure rates rocket up to 69 per cent when this work isn't done against 25–32 per cent when it is.

Those of us who have worked in strategy and planning will not be surprised by this finding, although it is definitely reassuring to see that common sense is reflected by proper statistical analysis. When projects start before the real thinking and evaluation is done, whether or not they have been given a detailed list of requirements, features and functions, they will tend to fail, and do so at a significantly higher rate than other projects.

A later Cooper study[17] goes further and suggests that having a 'well-defined' product is a vital determinant of timely product delivery, a key secondary factor.

---

17   As described in Cooper, R. 2001. *Winning at New Products*. Cambridge, MA: Perseus Books.

3. Technological synergy and quality

Technological synergy is a measure of how far from its current technology a firm must stray to build the product. The further away the firm strays, the less likely the project will be successful. Again the spread is broad: those in the top 20 per cent had an 80 per cent chance of success, those in the bottom 20 per cent had a 29 per cent chance.

Beyond synergy itself, although clearly influenced by it, is the quality of technological activities — still a major challenge for many businesses and one which significantly impacts success.

4. Marketing synergy and quality

How well is the product matched with the existing marketing machinery of the business? Again, a poor match spells trouble (the bottom 20 per cent experienced a failure rate of 70 per cent).

5. Market attractiveness

How big is the market and in what direction is it travelling? How important is the product to the market? If the product is a first of its kind, will consumers even get it?

Of course, very few products will get top marks in all of these areas. But where one or more of these factors is likely to be an issue for any reason — for example, because a company needs to work outside its technological comfort zone — it will become even more important that the other areas rank high.

How might we relate this analysis to the distinction between revolutionary and normal innovation? The key here is that at least two of the indicators of success — market and technical synergy and quality — are likely to be low. By definition, a revolutionary product will be outside of the core experience that a business has in at least one of these areas.

Taking the synergy factors out of the equation for the time being and not thinking for the moment about process and structure, we can now see that in fact there are only two things that matter. First, you must create a great product with a very clearly defined and large consumer market where the product resolves a real consumer issue and offers superb differentiation over its competitors. Secondly, the product must be well-defined across consumer, technology and business prior to full execution commencing.

So, for revolutionary products to overcome an inherent weakness in technology and marketing synergy, a new approach is needed that encourages learning through active engagement and experimenting with both what will work technically and with how the market might respond to the product.

6.1 Factors that don't correlate with success

What is perhaps just as interesting from the studies of new product development success are the factors which — it turns out — do not directly influence product success.

1. Top management support

Previous studies had highlighted the importance of executive support or the buy in of senior managers. Cooper found that in fact, top managers were as likely to support a failure as a success. And, that top management involvement was more likely to take to market projects that might otherwise be put out of their misery earlier on. Cooper's feel is that the executive should 'set the stage: commit to a game plan, and make available the right resources... day-to-day meddling and pushing projects by top management is not conducive to success'.

2. Market competitiveness

Although reported with less confidence than other items, Cooper and others have evidence that the competitiveness of the market into which the product is launched is not a strong determinant of likely success. If a product can still be differentiated, the competitiveness of the market itself is of surprisingly little consequence.

6.2 Thinking global from the outset

We've deliberately excluded from this discussion the question of making your products work in more than one market. The learning here is that products originally conceived for international markets are much more likely to succeed in multiple markets than those tried in one place and later extended to multiple markets.

Having multiple countries as potential markets also broadens the range of consumer problems that a product might seek to address. And, in that sense, it broadens the possibilities that can be explored, whilst also amplifying the challenge of understanding the human behaviours that will be at the heart of any successful product development.

Chapter 7

Making the
Unthinkable Thinkable

The solution we're proposing will not feel familiar. It also may not seem — at first — to be particularly easy to achieve. But it can be done and, once achieved, it will fundamentally alter the perspective of your entire organisation and its ability to do new things.

At its heart, the challenge is this: when attempting to make something new which is revolutionary, you must not just be creative with the product, you must have the ability to recalibrate the company to think about, and operate successfully in, a totally new market, or to think about an existing market in a totally new way. And, unlike your existing market, the new market may well not be well formed yet, and it almost certainly doesn't suit many of your company's existing operating procedures, practices or success metrics.

The identification of successful new products must, therefore, be based on the ability to actively understand new markets.

Think of all of the companies that have attempted to enter the digital music distribution market. Why is it that Apple succeeded where brands as diverse as HMV, Nokia, Tesco and numerous startups have so far failed to capture the imagination of consumers? Perhaps it was through the force of a very particular will. Perhaps it was through an incredible focus on the value of the change. Perhaps it was because Apple loves music. Or perhaps it was the opposite: it doesn't care terribly much about music and so avoid the traps previous music obsessives have fallen into. Either way, that company, which was previously a computer manufacturer, managed to completely reorient itself to a new market.

We know now of the success Apple achieved in doing this. And so it is less easy to understand quite how big a deal that transformation really was.

Apple perceived that, in the future, there would be a massive market for digitally downloaded music. It created a hardware and software product for the market which required the negotiation of extremely complicated rights and the establishment of a server infrastructure which was significantly beyond anything the company had previously achieved.

Apple brought the product to market with the same slick marketing it had exhibited for years in its other product lines, having identified a distinct consumer benefit of digital music — your entire music collection in your pocket.

Imagine what could have gone wrong. How many times do you think the product was challenged internally for not being a *core* business? How many staff questioned that consumers would ever learn to act in this way? How many suggested that the technology could not be achieved. How many, do you do think, suggested that the already very successful company should stick to its knitting?

Could your business do this? Would your staff let you? Would your customers?

We know the ingredients for new product success. We know the shape of a product that takes us beyond our current market. We know, too, the behaviours and factors which hold us back, and stop us making the necessary leap. How do we break those habits and deliver the next product success?

7.1 Our five principles for revolutionary innovation

1. Get the right idea before getting the idea right

Don't let the potential execution of your genius idea trample over identifying your genius idea in the first place.

It's tempting to have an idea, visualise how you think it would work as an end product, and get on with designing and building it, assuming that you have all the answers you need. However, by doing this, you may well not be capitalising on the opportunity or insight that led you to the idea in the first place. Or worse, your original insight might be completely invalid.

This is the homework mentioned earlier that is so important to the success of new products — ensuring you understand the essence of the idea, that the problem you are trying to solve, or the opportunity you are trying to exploit, actually exists — and then getting it into shape as a proposition that delivers on the promise of that idea. This means a proposition that meets the needs of customers, that is feasible to make, and viable to operate. Only then can you really think about the best possible execution.

Determining the essence of a product involves unravelling a proposed solution until you get you back to the core insight that led you to the idea in the first place. Once unravelled, you can clearly see the difference between idea and execution, and you can formulate that original idea as a hypothesis you can later test.

When you do this, your ideas about the execution usually change dramatically as you discover more about the value that the proposition has for end consumers and the feasibility and viability of the execution.

The desire to skip the proposition development phase and get straight into the production of that idea is a recipe for disaster. Desirability (will customers want it?), feasibility (can it be made?) and viability (can it make a profit?) must all be understood before you can decide on the execution and start building in earnest.

The proposition must, at this stage, tell you who you believe you are going to sell the product to, and how you are going to sell it; what are the distribution networks, who are the partners, how will your product be presented? You must have convincing hypotheses on whether or not customers will buy it, and what their choices and motivations are when they do.

2. Stop making predictions and start experimenting

Without a doubt, the number one cause of missed targets is the setting of targets.

The rule here is that if you've been asked by your boss to predict how successful your innovation will be, you are no longer in the innovation game.

You must avoid being pulled into predictive behaviour too early. Companies that require this sort of forecasting in the early stages of product development are doing nothing more sophisticated than asking to be lied to, albeit with complex-looking spreadsheets and graphs to support those lies.

We're not averse to a litmus test of viability in the shape of a rough calculation where you work out what constitutes a significant product in the world of your normal business, and working back to see whether it's feasible to build it at the right cost or to reach enough customers. But we stop short at making grand predictions of future success.

At Fluxx, we call this the 'Numbers Game': someone sets an arbitrary target of profit we want to achieve, and we work out how many sales or customers we would need to achieve this random — but compelling — number. What this process does not do is make any predictions; rather, it highlights what we don't know and shows us what things would have to be true to make us successful. It also allows us to sanity check our customer or sales requirements against other known businesses. This activity is not intended to be a predictive exercise or generate a business case; it is simply an activity that highlights the potential weak links in the chain we know we'll have to look at in more detail later. We are always careful not to allow these numbers to turn into targets or predictions.

As described in *The Other Side of Innovation* (p. 146), there is an interesting cognitive bias when targets are missed in business to assume that outcomes were too low, rather than the predictions too high.

What experimenting does is bring increasing levels of certainty to some of the numbers that underpin the calculations in our Numbers Game. A series of small experiments will steadily evolve your understanding of what something will actually take to deliver, how customers will react to it and, therefore, the likelihood of achieving the numbers you need to make the business stack up.

As our good friend Shed Simove says, 'experiments don't succeed or fail, they merely have outcomes'. Experiments will have hypotheses to test, for sure, but whether a hypothesis is validated or not should not be seen as a business target hit or missed but, rather, simply as something you've learned that will improve the product you're working on.

The 'big bets' culture has businesses agonising over, say, a £2m investment for a new product based on no actual evidence. Rather than take this one huge bet, the experimenting method proposes we take a series of much smaller bets, say twenty £100,000 bets, or even 200 £10,000 bets and, in the process, learn a massive amount about the market, the product and what is likely to work; and we do, of course, have the ability to stop at any time without losing face.

With these much smaller budgets, we free up more investment to explore more areas of opportunity, and also reduce the level of predictive promises that business teams require from each other in return for releasing that capital. Remember, the smaller the 'I', the less we care about the 'R' in ROI…

3. Learn from what people do, not what they say they will do

We know that we are bad at predicting how other people will behave. Why then would our customers be any better than us at predicting how they themselves will behave?

There is a fiction persisted by researchers that we can find out what people will do in the future, or indeed discover why they did something in the past, by simply asking them. What these methods don't account for is that people simply don't always tell the truth. They don't do it maliciously, but they craft responses to market research based on a complex set of very human considerations. How will my answer affect someone's perception of me? Will my answer prejudice some benefit to me or to my fellow humans at some point in the future? How would other people want me to answer? How can I look clever to the rest of the group? How does the researcher who paid me money and put a glass of wine in my hand want me to respond?

So we need to find new ways to find out what customers care about, and how they will actually react to the products we are developing.

4. Build a team to learn, not to 'succeed'

Probably best phrased by Jeremy Clark in *Pretotyping@work*[18] when he says: 'Wake up, Pollyanna: MOST NEW IDEAS FAIL.' Clark and his

---

18   Clark, J. 2012. *Pretotyping@work: Invent Like A Startup, Invest Like A Grownup.* Ebook: Pretotype Labs.

colleague, Alberto Savoia, also coin the brilliantly reversed catchphrase: 'Failure is an option.'

When you are in the incubation phase, the results of any experiments or study should not impact on the wellbeing of individuals or the team itself. The reality is that this can be very difficult to do. Left to their own devices, teams are very likely to become emotionally attached to the ideas on which they are working, and they are likely to make a connection between this idea and advancement in their careers. But the outcomes must impact on the idea itself and not on the team that learned of the outcomes — in other words, we must thank the messenger, not shoot them.

The measure of success and, therefore, the basis of rewards and advancement for the team must be their ability to learn, and to generate learning. We must reward our staff's own behaviours, and not the behaviour of the markets. If we incentivise our people to produce results, then they will bias themselves to find positive outcomes — regardless of what they have learned in the process about the suitability of the idea for our business. We should reward responsible, honest behaviour, as that's the only way we will know when it's right to start — or shut down — a project.

Get people used to moving on quickly with no stigma attached. As much discipline should be applied in de-funding projects as went into funding them in the first place. When shutting down a larger initiative, you need to take time to ensure the reasons are understood and retained, and that the team involved sees it as the right thing to do rather than as a reflection on its abilities. The advantage of having a centralised function that deals with new product development is that team members can retain the knowledge and learnings from everything, regardless of whether or not a product went to market. In addition, they can see every outcome, even a negative one, as acceptable, not as a personal failure.

And don't keep it a secret. The innovation team must get used to giving bad news as well as good. And the board (or whatever executive exists) must get used to receiving it. Unless you're incredibly lucky, there's going to be more bad news than good news coming. Attempts to conceal the bad news or magically transform it into good news are futile. Regular grown-up conversations are critical to a sane innovation process. They also provide a platform for the innovation team's work to be shared with the business which may of course make for some quite unexpected successes, through other parts of the business making use of what has been learned.

5. Do something

As you will discover very early on in any innovation programme you launch, the lists of reasons not to do something will always be longer than the list of reasons to do it. But not even attempting something is to admit defeat from the outset.

The number one characteristic of successful innovators is ongoing enthusiasm and tenacity. Without any success or failure, there is nothing to learn from, just a void — a total lack of knowledge or information. Doing something will start to fill that void with evidence rather than opinions and increase your confidence about what to do next. Leaving the void empty will paralyse you.

7.1.1 Getting the right product

Taken to its most extreme and somewhat unhelpful simplicity, creating an amazing new product or service has three key stages:

1. Figuring out a great product which has an identifiable market and can be produced at a profit;
2. Executing it flawlessly;

3. Finding ways to make it better, incorporating feedback from the marketplace.

When we are in stage one, we are learning about a market, learning about technology and assessing business viability. That is all.

If you don't do stage one right, then the rest of the process is irrelevant. Stage one is neither the most time consuming nor the most labour intensive.

But it is the most uncomfortable. Most people have no idea what it feels like to do it. The last time they had to work this way, they were in kindergarten, trying to build a picture out of bits of straw. And so they feel uncomfortable doing this sort of thing in the office.

Of course, for the most part, the instinct to not act like you are in a kindergarten in the office is the right one. But to do this first stage well means changing your understanding of what is appropriate in a corporate environment. We think this is why people find it hard.

If the idea is not evaluated then no amount of peerless execution or customer feedback at the end of the day will fix it. So we're stuck with the need to do this uncomfortable bit.

Indeed, this is the bit that startups find so natural. When you're starting with nothing, all you can really do is experiment to see what works and what doesn't. You have limited resources and so you do what is within your power and budgets to do in order to advance your understanding.

Some have interpreted the 'Lean Startup' movement as being about maximum possible speed to market, and others have interpreted the concept of a 'minimum viable product' as meaning that we should go to market with the bare minimum of features in order to balance our investment with risk.

But this is not what Eric Ries actually describes in *The Lean Startup* — and both ideas are very dangerous. That's not to say that

Ries and the lean movement don't emphasise pace. What Ries observed was that lean startups were unafraid to get into their markets quickly in order to generate some learnings. They got inexpensive experiments out really fast into the real world to see how people reacted, and it's these experiments which are used to evaluate their hypotheses about what would make their product successful.

They did it this way precisely because they knew that to build a product worthy of launch to consumers would be expensive and time-consuming in order for them to get it right — no matter how bare its feature-set.

If we go to market now, even with a bare version of the whole product, then we are jumping to stage two. We have moved from evaluation to implementation. And if we then chose to launch something half-featured, we are not doing stage two properly either. Stage two says we should make the product as good as it can be. A product missing half the eventual features is not as good as it could be.

So, we agree with Ries; that we should first evaluate various hypotheses about the product as we proceed, with just enough investment to get the learning we desire about what will make a successful end product.

With this approach, our hope is that a whole series of features or facets will never have to be developed — badly or otherwise — as we discover that they are simply not required to drive the value implicit in our product, and instead we learn which elements of the product particularly matter to the customer.

Getting the right product is as much about learning about the viability of our product as it is about understanding its value in the market. Just how hard will it be to produce, or to operate? Could we make it better by adding more, or perhaps by taking more away?

We should be learning, too, about our routes to market. Who will help us to sell our product? Who will help us to distribute it? Can a partner make it easier or cheaper to produce? What other tools, partners or technologies would make it better?

7.1.2 Stop making predictions

> 'History is merely a list of surprises.
> It can only prepare us to be surprised yet again.'
> —**Kurt Vonnegut**[19]

The most important single duty of a manager of a new product development team is to avoid the temptation to make bold predictions. And, similarly, as a director of an enterprise where innovation is critical, avoid creating a culture of arbitrary prediction making.

As we've said before, not all normal business is predictable. In 2011, a tsunami in Japan caused power and component shortages in the region that directly impacted upon industrial output and global corporate profitability. In October 2012, flooding in Manhattan caused the so-called capital of the world to shut down for three days in a row.

However, most businesses function on the basis of repeatability and predictability. It is when we are trying to learn about new things that we need to admit we don't know what will happen. It is only habit that would have us do otherwise. If lack of knowledge is the problem, then learning has to be the solution, not guessing.

And how do we learn about things? Again, the answers are almost childishly simple:

1. We find someone who knows the answers; or
2. We experiment.

---

19   Vonnegut, K. 1991. *Slapstick*. London: Vintage.

	Someone else has done it before	Someone else hasn't done it before
You have done it before	Normal	Normal
You haven't done it before	Hire the person who has done it before and experiment	Experiment

Even in a scenario where it feels like others *should* know the answer to the question and, indeed, where you manage to find someone who has done something similar in the past, it is important to acknowledge differences that can exist because of brands, target markets, or even timing with the product you are trying to develop.

7.1.2.1 Testing commercial viability

Commercial viability is — in many ways — the easiest of the constraints to understand. It is certainly the area with the most established practice.

By the time you seek large-scale funding to bring your idea to life, you will need to have a very well-considered financial business plan for the new product or business. But that time is not now. Far too often, innovators put off making an initial plan because they are intimidated by the task, fearing they will be falling short by not producing a masterwork on first draft.

But this is not how it works. Like the product itself, and your level of knowledge of the market, the business plan will develop as you progress. It's great to look back at successful ideas and companies we have seen come to market and see how the business planning evolved with them.

A basic business plan can be constructed in just a few hours. Doing your first plan will make you feel a great deal more confident about building more comprehensive plans in future. And it will also force you to focus on some key factors which will inform every other aspect of the plan. Start here.

There are numerous approaches to building business plans. We typically use the business model canvas (see http://www. businessmodelgeneration.com/canvas). We'll talk in a little bit more detail about actually carrying this out later, and how it feeds into a commercial model.

However, the most important part of doing this for the first time is to force yourself to answer the following questions:

1. Who is the potential customer for this product?
2. What problem do they have that this product will solve?
3. How will my product solve their problem?
4. What other solutions are there for this customer problem?
5. How does my solution compare to these solutions (if any)?
6. How much would a customer be willing to pay for this?

And now you've got your hypotheses, you can play the Numbers Game, and sketch out a plan for how you'll make money from each customer. It doesn't have to be rocket science. But if you can't make it work on the back of a napkin, what chance have you got in the marketplace?

As we said earlier, if you have big holes in this plan (or significant costs that you can't see how to overcome), what you've done is simply set out some of your risks and assumptions that you need to find out more about later.

What else have you learned?

In thinking about such a fundamental structure of your business, you have also begun to state the most basic assumptions you are making. These assumptions will prove to be the real questions you must understand to make a success of the idea. Begin to get into the habit of recording every one and then finding a way to address it before proceeding to the next step. Every assumption you keep unchecked as you move forward is a risk. It could be the thing that kills your progress later. So keep a list.

7.1.2.2 Modelling complex businesses

Complexity can arise in many ways. But often it comes from the need to try and understand the conditional usage of a product. So, for example, it may be easy to model the financial viability of selling an online storage service where a customer pays a fixed rate to gain access to the service, but more complex to model the business where usage impacts pricing, or some element of the service is available for free in the long term as a promotion for the service.

The disadvantage for the entrepreneur or new business team is that companies that have managed to make a success of these complex business models (such as the very darling of the lean startup world: Dropbox) do not talk about their model publicly. And, even when they do, these statements must be taken with a massive pile of salt.

The only way to learn to about these more complex, conditional models typically is to construct your own models and then conduct experiments to understand how people might react in them.

We won't go into the detailed construction of models here, but we do have a few key pointers:

1. Build models so that they have as many parameters as possible. In working on one project, we were able to determine that certain styles of pricing would never work using the business model alone, by showing that even with the most optimistic customer forecast case, long-term usage growth would result in a negative margin.

2. Be careful who the models are shared with. They could be taken as predictions, which could be potentially fatal for the project. Typically, it will be possible to adjust assumptions (parameters) to create positive and negative outcomes. If you must save or distribute the files, do so with the negative or break-even scenarios, lest your plans be misused as a yardstick of future performance.

3. It is easy to miss costs. This creates excessively optimistic models. Address this by including an additional cost line which can be set to inflate costs arbitrarily by up to 100 per cent.

4. It is easy to miss revenues or other positive effects. For example, there may be opportunities to gain revenue from advertising in an online service. Make sure that these are included but take precautions to ensure that they're not the elements that justify the investment.

5. Forecast as far out as possible (typically five years). We have seen several unusual business cases that flip after 12–18 months. Very few of today's most successful products made a positive return in the first 12 or even 24 months (including Facebook and Twitter) yet, bizarrely, very few companies are willing to even begin to invest in product ideas which don't achieve positive returns in this timescale. This is where your company's current attitudes towards investment and reporting might well be challenged.

6. Beware of impossible growth forecasts. Anyone can build growth projects that do not have an effective limiting factor. For example, imagine you start out with 1,000 customers in month one for a volleyball TV subscription service and then increase the users by a factor of 1.3 (i.e. month two is 1,300, month three is 1,690, and so on). This might seem reasonable. Bear in mind, however, that by month 60 (the end of year five), you

will be forecasting 0.5 million subscribers. Are there really that many volleyball fans in your market? And are you going to be able to attract them all? Downward pressure on growth comes from market penetration. But this is the posh way of saying use your common sense when building models, and marry them up to real-world statistics about your market.

7. Free earns you nothing and teaches you nothing. The behaviour of customers around 'free' has long been studied. Nothing you learn about customer behaviour with a free product will teach you anything about a paid-for product, so don't expect that a product researched as free can be migrated to a paid-for price point.

8. Market viability is not necessarily portable *between* markets. For example, the economics of the top end of the market will be very different from the economics at the bottom. Geographically disparate markets, especially those with different competitor sets, will behave quite differently and need to be independently assessed.

We think of such models like lines of code in a digital prototype or the wires hanging out of a physical test device. They help us to understand how the product will live in the market, as we understand how a user will react to a visual or physical prompt.

Try to model so that you can understand dynamics rather than predict them.

7.1.2.3 Acceptable margins for big companies

A key question to ask when drawing up models to test 'viability' is: what would count as an acceptable margin or return for a product?

This question hides a more complex consideration, which is that the market and, therefore, margin for new products can evolve over time.

So early versions of a product may have a small market and low margins, but as these markets develop both margins and size can improve.

From this point of view, the business may potentially need to be able to operate in the market at a small scale and / or low margin in order to reap the benefits. The clearest example of this dichotomy is given in Christensen's analysis of the Apple Newton. He makes the point that when Apple's first products (such as the Apple II) were developed, sales of just a few thousand low-margin units were regarded as a major victory. Enough, in fact, to generate a very highly-rated listing of the company itself. By the time the Newton came to market, Apple had to achieve much more (despite launching the product into a market every bit as immature as the personal computing market had been 15 years earlier). So much so that the Newton was seen as a failure:

'It was a market-creating, disruptive product targeted at an undefinable set of users whose needs were unknown to either themselves or Apple. On that basis, Newton's sales should have been a pleasant surprise to Apple's executives: It outsold the Apple II in its first two years by a factor of more than three to one. But while selling 43,000 units was viewed as an IPO-qualifying triumph in the smaller Apple of 1979, selling 140,000 Newtons was viewed as a failure in the giant Apple of 1994.'[20]

It is not just that companies are selling to early adopters; it may well be that the eventual purpose of the innovation is not its originally intended purpose. And, in fact, such clarity can come only from a time-consuming cycle of trial and modification in the market itself. Judged by the rules of the parent company, such programmes may be deemed to have failed too early as the energy needed to sustain them to fruition may simply be absent from an organisation that is used to greater

20   Christensen, C. 1997. *The Innovator's Dilemma.* Cambridge, MA: Harvard Business School Press, p.131.

predictability and larger day-to-day successes. And this is the reason that a new, hungrier startup may find it easier to prosper.

This game of comparisons is very clearly an example of why large companies often pull out of innovation ventures whilst startup companies continue aggressively pursuing the same market. And it is a core reason why we believe any innovation team must be isolated from the management of its parent company in a meaningful way. That's not to say that new businesses should be massive loss-makers of course, but that they cannot operate to the margins honed over years by their parents, just as graduates can't be expected to immediately earn a salary the size of their parents'.

7.1.3 Learn from what people do

Now we need to find out whether there is a market for our product, and what the dynamics of that market are. This will be the hardest and most important question to answer.

We have a very simple belief about this area of learning: when it comes to assessing whether consumers will purchase a product or service, the only strong predictor will be whether they have actually done it before. Therefore, to learn about whether a product is likely to be a success from a customer point of view means finding a way to put the product in front of potential purchasers and getting them to react to it as if it were real.

What we must not do is rely on asking customers to *predict* what their behaviour will be (without seeing something); neither must we try to infer likely customer behaviour by observing a different product in a different market.

As Christensen says:

'Markets that do not exist cannot be analysed: Suppliers and customers must discover them together. Not only are the market

applications for disruptive technologies unknown *at the time of their development, they are* unknowable. *The strategies and plans that managers formulate for confronting disruptive technological change therefore should be plans for learning and discovery rather than plans for execution. This is an important point to understand because managers who believe they know a market's future will plan and invest very differently from those who recognise the uncertainties of a developing market.'*[21]

He continues: 'Guessing the right strategy at the outset isn't nearly as important to success as conserving enough resources (or having the relationships with trusting backers or investors) so that new business initiatives get a second or third stab at getting it right.'[22]

7.1.3.1 What people say, and what they do

'In the mid-1990s Michael Moore's TV show pioneered a post-modern playfulness with dumb research event polls ("46 per cent of Americans said they would rather be killed by a serial killer than by a mass murderer").'[23]

We need to learn about how a potential market may react to a new product, under what circumstances consumers might buy it, how much they might be prepared to pay for it, and so on.

This is a very lucrative business. In the UK, £1.3bn is spent annually on market research. In the US, the number is over £11bn. In the UK, one study by the Department of Health alone cost more than £11m.

In his book, *Consumer.ology*,[24] Philip Graves argues that all, not just a proportion, of this money is wasted. Asking people to describe what

21   Christensen, C. 1997. *The Innovator's Dilemma.* Cambridge, MA: Harvard Business School Press, p.143.
22   Ibid, p.151.
23   Lannon J. and Baskin M. (eds) 2007. *A Master Class in Brand Planning: The Timeless Works of Stephen King.* Chichester: Wiley, p.43.
24   Graves, P. 2010. *Consumer.ology: The Market Research Myth, the Truth about Consumer Behaviour and the Psychology of Shopping.* London: Nicholas Brealey Publishing.

they have done in the past, do today or will do in the future is — he believes — very ineffective at actually understanding what people do or will do.

There's a lot of evidence that he is right.

What we have seen is that there is a world of difference between what people say they will do, and what they actually do.

Why is this?

Because answering questions for a researcher is a fundamentally different thing to actually making decisions. Asking research participants to respond rationally is not asking them to respond as they will in the market place because we are very often not rational in our own decision making, and very often we simply do not understand how we have arrived at own decisions.

In a research context, respondents will try appear as if they have a clear and consistent decision-making process, even though the evidence suggests that decision making is — in reality — of a much more visceral nature.

To confuse matters, respondents will often post-rationalise their decision — explaining the 'reasons' for their actions to an attentive researcher, an effect that will be compounded in a group setting.

The respondent does not want to appear like someone crazily making decisions on impulse as if afflicted with a weird form of retail Tourette's. And so the accounts of making decisions are sanitised and post-rationalised to create a disarmingly lucid account of a *process* which never actually occurred, a beautifully constructed fiction intended to impress the researcher and other participants, while helping the subjects feel as though they are capable of highly coherent thought rather than being a creature of uncontrollable urges and whims.

Graves cites a University of Virginia study where respondents were asked to select their favourite of four pairs of tights (pantyhose). Having made their selections, participants gave explanations ranging from sheerness to knit to elasticity, although — in fact — all four products were identical.

This is not the only serious flaw in traditional *ask the customer* research methods.

If the research has been commissioned to validate decisions already made, and the researcher is actively seeking evidence to move the project forward, just how much of what is being said is really being listened to?

When judging desirability, we are faced with a further and equally intractable challenge.

Humans are very poor at predicting how cost will affect their decisions. 'I would like to offset my impact on the environment' and 'I am in favour of eradicating world hunger' are both difficult statements to disagree with in the absence of an actual, tangible cost. Do you know anyone who is not for the eradication of hunger? Now try knocking on their door and asking for a donation towards the world food programme.

The ability for research to misjudge the likely commercial reception for a product works both ways. Over the years many products, including Bailey's Irish Cream and the Aeron Chair were rejected by focus groups but embraced by real-life customers. Once again, customers are found to be unable to predict how they will actually respond to the product when they meet it for real, and when they experience not just the product itself, but its marketing and the reaction that others have to it.

Perhaps one of the most famous examples of product research failing to predict market reaction is New Coke and the challenge they were facing from Pepsi. Malcolm Gladwell points out that when people are asked to sip a cola, they are naturally inclined to prefer a sweeter taste but that they do not maintain this preference when drinking the cola regularly and in larger quantities. So Gladwell argues that this is why people favoured Pepsi in blind taste tests, yet consumers reacted badly when Coca Cola shifted their formula to be more like Pepsi.

Greeves has a more radical theory. His view is that the research stood as much chance as being wrong as it did of being right since those sampled were intrinsically unable to predict market reaction to the change itself.

In either case, it seems there is a case to be argued that those who liked the taste of New Coke would probably not prefer it as dramatically as those who disliked the changed formulation — either for taste reasons or because they are simply change-averse — and that this group were always bound to be more vocal. In fact, the research could have predicted this — since the same effect was seen in the groups — but Coca-Cola failed to interpret such a response as significant.

Another Gladwell example is coffee. In his 2006 TED talk on taste,[25] Gladwell says: 'The mind knows not what the tongue wants. [...] If I asked all of you, for example, in this room, what you want in a coffee, you know what you'd say? Every one of you would say "I want a dark, rich, hearty roast". It's what people always say when you ask them what they want in a coffee. What do you like? Dark, rich, hearty roast! What percentage of you actually like a dark, rich, hearty roast? According to Howard [a consumer taste test specialist], somewhere between 25 and 27 per cent of you. Most of you like milky, weak coffee. But you will never, ever say to someone who asks you what you want — that "I want a milky, weak coffee".'

For all the talk of Steve Jobs' *focus group of one* at Apple, his attitude was in fact that you need to understand who your customer is, what their life is like and what they would love to be able to do with technology. Using this information allowed Apple to innovate and design phenomenally successful products. As he said in *Fortune Magazine* in January 2000:

'This is what customers pay us for — to sweat all these details so it's easy and pleasant for them to use our computers. We're supposed to be

25   http://www.ted.com/talks/malcolm_gladwell_on_spaghetti_sauce.html

really good at this. That doesn't mean we don't listen to customers, but it's hard for them to tell you what they want when they've never seen anything remotely like it. Take desktop video editing. I never got one request from someone who wanted to edit movies on his computer. Yet now that people see it, they say, "Oh my God, that's great!" '

So, what are the key lessons for research?

1. Don't use research to design your product, do it to investigate your customer and understand them better.
2. Don't use research to prove you are right. It always will. Instead try to find a question or hypothesis you can learn something about and be very careful to remove as many biases as possible from the experiment.
3. Don't expect participants to predict the future or remember accurately why they did something in the past.
4. Don't believe the reasons people gave you in research to explain their decisions and actions.
5. Beware research taken to delay an action or decision, often senior exec will call for research to be undertaken not to learn more but to confuse and slow down a process that they don't buy into. If someone wanted to kill Jobs' video editing software they would have commissioned research simply asking 'How often are you likely to edit videos at home?'
6. Be very careful about which kinds of research you carry out. In particular, there are two types of research of which we are extremely cautious, even though they are very commonly used in the development of new products;

7.1.3.1.1 Focus groups

The idea behind a focus group is pretty straightforward. You recruit a bunch of people who match a set of qualifying criteria. You get them together and you ask their opinions about the market segment you are interested in, or about a product you have developed. The participants in the study are able to interact with each other. Whilst this interplay can occasionally create issues with moderation of the group, it is typically seen as a positive, allowing participants to develop their viewpoints.

A traditional approach is to show early designs / prototypes of a product in such a focus group setting, and ask users to provide feedback.

While focus groups may be very valuable for other things, we are not confident in their ability to help us either understand potential customers or test new products. In terms of understanding customers, we find focus groups unreliable because of the impact the group dynamic has on people's behaviour. Unless you are creating a product inherently geared to groups (for example, a restaurant format), customers do not make the decisions in such a group context. Yes, they are certainly influenced by friends and relatives but not in the quite the same, self-conscious way that people react with others in focus groups.

But it is in product testing that groups are particularly unhelpful. For the reasons outlined in the previous section, our experience is that customers do not really know how they feel about new products when presented with them in this context.

So, asking them this question is unlikely to create reliable results. Instead, you are likely to get results to the experiment *What happens when you ask members of the public to act like product designers?* There may be some useful outputs from the exercise but it will not answer the question — will people buy or use this product?

As Steve Jobs himself said: 'In the end, for something this complicated, it's really hard to design products by focus groups. A lot of times, people don't know what they want until you show it to them.'[26]

---

26   As quoted in *BusinessWeek* (25 May 1998); see http://www.businessweek.com/bwdaily/dnflash/may1998/nf80512d.htm

We would go one step further than that, simply showing people the product and asking for a hypothetical reaction may provide different results from putting the product in their hands in a non-research setting. Such an approach also lacks any of the influence of marketing and prior information which customers are presented with in the market, making it — at best — half a test.

7.1.3.1.2 Usability testing

The field of usability testing has come an incredibly long way since the early 1980s. Researchers can now reliably find usability issues and even — using new techniques such as ECG scans — figure out where products particularly challenge, stress or delight a user. In such tests, the user's ability to achieve a set of tasks will be assessed. For example, the user may be asked to find a piece of information, or purchase a particular product on a website, or use a physical or electronic product in some way.

Such apparently simple tests can often reveal the most surprising flaws which had previously been invisible to those involved in a product's development. Their results are as valid for new products as they are for products that have been around for years, however, don't use usability testing to ask the wrong questions.

What usability tests provide is information about whether the user is able to make the product work in the way the inventor intended. That's all well and good, but we can't in this process also look for information about whether the user would *choose* to use the product in the first place. There is no point developing a highly usable product that no one wants.

Usability testing, therefore, has a role in the late stages of product development, and not to answer the big fundamental questions of stage one.

There seem to be three reasons why focus groups and usability testing have become popular in product development:

1. They are relatively inexpensive and easy to understand. Marketers in particular will be used to using these techniques.

2. They are relatively easy to rig — either through influence or interpretation and either deliberately or otherwise. We have many times seen the outputs of such groups dismissed when negative for the most spurious of reasons. Particularly in focus groups, we have seen senior marketers — slightly sozzled behind the two-way mirror — mocking their customers on the other side of the glass for failing to understand the product or promotion being 'assessed'.

3. The hammer and nail issue. If the agency you hire to research a product has a user testing lab and a focus group room, does the likelihood of these techniques being recommended increase? Even more likely to bias the research methodology are the skills of the researchers and the techniques they are most comfortable deploying.

In fact, we see this bias in research regularly. As Rory Sutherland puts it with the apocryphal story of the drunk and the lamppost:

'We have all heard the adage about people who use research as a drunk uses a lamppost — for support rather than illumination. Yet there is a better story about drunks and lampposts that David Ogilvy used to tell. A drunk had lost his keys on the street and was frantically searching for them under a streetlamp. "Where did you drop them?" asked a concerned passer-by. "Over there," he replied, indicating a spot 30 yards away. "So why are you looking here under the lamp?" "The light is better here." ' [27]

---

27 Lannon J. and Baskin M. (eds) 2007. *A Master Class in Brand Planning: The Timeless Works of Stephen King*. Chichester: Wiley, p.43.

7.1.3.2 Testing feasibility

Once we have a product we think customers will love, we may need to solve some problems relating to the feasibility of making it. A little like the imperfect customer prototypes and experiments we have just described, the key feature of technical prototypes should be that we focus on what we are trying to learn about, ensuring that we don't just try and rush to build an imperfect version of the product with each element or feature ten per cent complete.

For any project, there will be technical elements which we believe can be fairly easily tackled, and — conversely — those which are entirely new to us, or may seem at first to be utterly impossible.

We need to avoid working on the former — rebuilding things we've done 100 times in the past — although this may be tempting because these tasks seem much easier and less daunting than the areas we're trying to explore.

One such Fluxx project is a haptic (sensory-driven) navigation system which started life as a project called 'Buzz Gloves'. The concept is simple. Could we prompt people to walk, run, cycle or drive correctly to a destination by giving them small haptic hints, such as gloves which subtly vibrate. There's plenty of room to remove the actual gloves idea later (maybe putting the vibrating signals in something like bicycle handlebars) if required but this was an easy and memorable way to construct the product.

In the first prototype, all we wanted to learn is what it would feel like to have gloves on which mysteriously vibrated, and whether such an invention would be welcomed or despised by the wearer.

There are lots of bits of this that we could have built: internet connectivity, positioning, direction, decision making, user interface for setting up the route and so on. But would we learn anything by building these things, other than how clever and experienced we are?

Instead, we focused on doing the absolute bare minimum to test the idea.

Well, not quite the bare minimum. At one stage it was suggested that the test subject would walk along the street being followed by the 'navigator'. The navigator would have a long stick and would tap the test subject on either the left or right hand, depending on which way they should turn.

Now this test would have worked but we felt the weirdness of being struck with a stick in the street would make any other feeling or sensation difficult to detect. Instead, the team built a super-simple remote-control rig. Using an abandoned remote-control helicopter, a few wires and the vibrators from a pair of dancing hamster greetings cards, we made it possible for the navigator to vibrate the gloves of the test subject remotely.

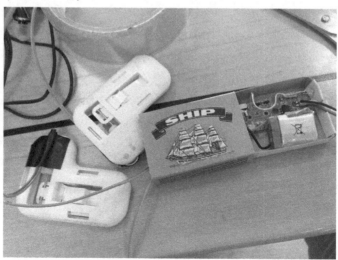

We used this simple set up a number of times to control subjects walking in and around the St Paul's area of London, near where our office was at the time. With hindsight, the appearance of a person walking aimlessly around the Old Bailey (the UK criminal court reserved for the most serious crimes) with wires hanging out of their back pocket may not have been the wisest choice, although perhaps better than the person being apparently beaten with a stick.

The experiment was very useful, it cost virtually nothing and we were up and running in less than half a day. The tools ended up in the office bin. This is inevitable. The key is making sure they were inexpensive in the first place. Again, reducing the 'I' in ROI to its absolute minimum.

7.1.3.3 Dealing with conflicting results

We've painted a picture here of a very predictable set of tests and interactions.

Of course, the reality is far from predictable, and the three types of learning are often interdependent.

In looking into consumer desirability, we will often need to radically rethink our technical questions or business model. Technical tests will rapidly impact on viability, and so on.

So, again, it will be important to maintain imagination and flexibility, as well as logic, throughout the process.

7.1.4 Build a team to learn

7.1.4.1 Personalities

Let us describe the ideal person for an innovation project. It is someone who likes to learn, someone who is not afraid to try new things and someone who does not become obsessively attached to their own ideas. It's someone who can bear others to be successful in a project team, and who is not afraid to rapidly change what they are doing. Depending on what area you are working in, it may well also be someone who has certain specific domain or technical skills.

There shouldn't be a shortage of people who can fill these roles. But that's not to say that we shouldn't focus in on the most suitable for this work. Should the opportunity to be involved in new product development be sought after in the business? Absolutely. But it should also be within the grasp of all those you value most in your workforce or, preferably, all those on your workforce.

It should certainly not be the preserve of the most ruthless ascenders of the greasy pole, the alpha males and females who rack up accomplishments inside in the organisation. Indeed, the need for openness and acceptance of the ideas of others eliminates exactly these corporate climbers. On many occasions, we've seen those from the factory floor or frontline of customer service be just as, or more, capable of providing useful input into the process.

7.1.4.2 Picking a project leader

Often, a team will have a project coordinator or manager whose role it is to organise things and remove issues that the project team is facing (sometimes referred to as 'blockers', a term from lean software engineering). This is not the leader. The leader is the person who chooses what the team will pursue, when they will change direction, how they will map out their progress and what they need to learn. The leader is also the person who must report progress to executives. It is the role that must constantly educate a variety of audiences about why the approach is being followed, effectively selling the approach to the organisation. More often than not, it will be this person who needs to safeguard the project from the parent organisation wishing to revert to form (especially in terms of forecasting, budgeting, outcomes and management).

So, it's a role that demands experience of the parent business, faith in the approach (without sight of the outcome), an ability to convince and motivate both senior stakeholders and the team themselves, and the ability to report positively on outcomes that may be regarded as negative.

Often, the behaviours associated with alpha managers who progress quickly in large organisations are sharply at odds with such a role, in particular with the ability to associate themselves with outcomes which some would determine to be failures.

In short, it is a particularly demanding role and one which does not automatically sit well with the sorts of people who do well in more traditional large businesses.

For this reason, we often find that the role will be best taken initially by an outsider with significant industry expertise but who has likely gained that from other companies and partners. Alternatively, the leader may be a relative newcomer to the business who is yet to learn about all the things that other staff regard as impossible. Here, the challenge becomes ensuring that this non-insider can command executive credibility, and ensuring that the team themselves respects and follows this leader.

7.1.4.3 Rational versus imaginative

Rory Sutherland, the enigmatic and expansive Vice Chairman of Ogilvy Group once said:

'Sutherland's first law states that "All creative people must submit their thinking for appraisal by more rational people". The second law states that "This does not apply the other way round".'[28]

He goes on to suggest that some of the dumbest decisions in the history of the world have been made because of the lack of creative, not rational, thought in the process. The observation is well merited.

'... I sincerely believe that a relentless application of logic, untempered by imagination is responsible for the greatest absurdities and extravagances we see in business and government. The [UK]

---

28 Lannon J. and Baskin M. (eds) 2007. *A Master Class in Brand Planning: The Timeless Works of Stephen King.* Chichester: Wiley, p.43.

3G [bandwidth] auction; NHS target-setting; the ERM [European Exchange Rate Mechanism] debacle; obsessive punctuality targets for trains — all have been perpetrated by people following the relentless dictates of logic without an imaginative grasp of the alternatives. And logic — unlike creativity — is allowed to go unpoliced.'[29]

The correct application of creativity in innovation is the subject of much debate but it is clear at least that the creative process begins, not ends, with the creation of powerful ideas.

What we have learned is that the idea behind a revolutionary innovation is only the seed of the final product that may or may not succeed in the market. It is the detail of the proposition and execution which, more often than not, will define the product's success. The ability to make more, to add, to rethink, to reset and restart, rather than to slash features and aim for the tried and tested, is so often the hallmark of genuinely exciting innovation.

Because there is no real coherent answer to the question 'how did you come up with that?' creativity can all too often disappear entirely from the accounts of how successful innovation was achieved. Again, case histories have their role in this distortion.

Sir Ken Robinson, an educator and public speaker, has it right in his analysis that education and business can try and kill creative thinking in favour of the rational and scientific. The skills we all are born with, the things we all do naturally when we are small children are gradually beaten out of us: 'Imagination is the source of every form of human achievement. And it's the one thing that I believe we are systematically jeopardising in the way we educate our children and ourselves.'[30]

A team that is likely to succeed will have a good mix of creative and analytical minds, as well as a healthy tension and respect between the two. Bear in mind that these two thinking modes are not mutually

---

29   Ibid
30   https://www.youtube.com/watch?v=iG9CE55wbtY

exclusive in individuals and you won't often have teams you can reliably sort into two discernible groups.

Free from the *traditional* bias of business management towards the rational over the imaginative, all too often, the teams will re-impose the restriction on themselves when they start to think about how the rest of the business will perceive them. It is the job of the project leader to keep that tension running.

7.1.4.4 Allow them to act responsibly

Let's get one thing clear. There is absolutely no way that a product team will be successful unless the team members involved all act responsibly. This shouldn't be surprising. As we set sail in our new venture, we will be short-staffed and faced with enormous challenges. We will need to do a lot with a little. We simply can't afford to waste time nor add additional unpredictability.

This shouldn't be too difficult to achieve. In our experience, it is the average person's default position. Most of us don't start work with our political skills finely honed. We learn these somewhat counterproductive skills over time. The opportunity to shed these concerns is liberating. But in order to do so, we must create a work environment where the essentially defensive measures of office politics are not required.

So status, reward and job security need to be taken out of the equation. Of course, this is more easily said than done. We will need to make some promises:

1. The innovation project is like a maternity leave, but for ideas not offspring. The team will return to their day jobs, or better. That is to say, if they so choose they can go back to the roles they previously held on the same salary, benefits and status. The foray into innovation is a temporary one, at the staff

members' discretion. A project failure must not necessarily represent a personal failure, so it should not have a negative personal outcome.

2. Should the team receive a salary bump for joining the new business project? Our view is no. It should be an opportunity in and of itself, not one for which financial incentive is needed. By removing the potential downsides of the secondment, we make such lateral moves more attractive.

3. To reduce jostling, it is typically best to remove concepts of status as far as possible from the team. Luckily, small teams don't need a lot of structure, just one leader. Focusing on the leader's ability to motivate, lead and manage disparate skills is therefore key.

4. We've already mentioned that the staff should not be rewarded based on the outcomes of their work. Rather they should (singularly and collectively) be rewarded for their behaviour in the project such as asking intelligent questions, effective design of experiments, clear interpretation of results and the ability to confidently answer 'I don't know' when asked to make crazy predictions.

5. As far as possible, reduce the process to small, self-contained projects. The leader of a project or group of projects should be able to redeploy teams depending on the skills of individuals and how well they work together.

6. Have clear plans up front for what will happen if the current stream succeeds or fails in gaining the green light to progress. If you don't do this, staff will invent their own outcomes. For example, if our plan means that the team will go back to their day jobs if the project produces a negative outcome, we may have inadvertently created an incentive to carry on with the work longer than necessary or to interpret the results in

too favourable a light. Perhaps it is better to have staff move on to the next stream if this one has shown it will not work. This provides a strong motivation to report findings quickly and honestly.

7. Put in place a clear management structure for the teams in question. In particular, while employees are on the team, they will be subject to management by demonstration of values, rather than management by results. The result of a disciplinary action would be a return to the previous role, and would remain on their long-term records. This is the sort of failure we care about, and it should be very clearly separated from the perceived failure of speculative new products.

8. The values and behaviours targeted can be: generating and documenting learnings; sharing of learnings in the team; avoidance of the political behaviours; being on time and the reputation of the team itself in the wider business. At some distance, this may seem obvious, but up close it rarely is. Incentivise the behaviours that are likely to result in success, and that's it.

Success in the innovation stream (by behaviour) should be rewarded on the return to the regular business if the project closes.

7.1.4.5 Prepare them for failure

> *'Success is the ability to go from failure to failure without losing your enthusiasm.'*
> **—Winston Churchill**

> *'Everybody has a plan until they get punched in the mouth.'*
> **—Mike Tyson**

Much has been made of the ability to fail fast and of the likelihood of encountering many so-called failures before eventually hitting upon a success. That said, you don't really want to make a habit out of failure. Rather we must redefine what it means to fail. As with the Churchill quote above, the concept that we don't not fail but rather learn is not a new one. Edison famously said: 'I have not failed. I've just discovered 10,000 ways that won't work.'

Resilience, determination and a positive attitude are key. And that means, as an employer or leader, you must provide reinforcing structures for this sort of approach and attitude. From every negative experiment outcome, we must make sure we learn, either improving the idea we are evaluating or the evaluation process itself. The only crime should be learning the same lessons twice, or not learning them at all. As it is expressed in *The Other Side of Innovation* (p. 18): '[...], the innovator's job cannot be to deliver a proven result; it must be to discover what is possible, that is, to learn, by converting assumptions into knowledge as quickly and inexpensively as possible.'

While detailed project planning is very important once we commence design and build, and even more important in making an idea work in production, too much of an assumption about what planning can bring you is virtually a liability. Again in *The Other Side of Innovation* (p. 99), this is expressed very clearly: '... the competitor that wins is rarely the one with the best initial plan; it is the one that learns the fastest.'

7.1.4.6 Insiders or outsiders?

At first glance, candidates from inside the business should always be a better bet for innovation teams — they know the business, what they learn will be easier to retain, and they may even look cheaper than outside candidates. On the reverse of that equation, once we've put in place the considerations mentioned above, are they really cheaper for the project? Will it be easier for outsiders to see the possibilities in new ventures or to worry less about maintaining existing job roles and the general status quo? And couldn't outsiders who prove their worth be eventually converted to insiders?

The answer is that a mix of insiders and outsiders is best. Some may even be temporary inclusions in the team (such as outsiders from a company like Fluxx). But a great deal of care is needed here, around mixed incentives and conflict of interests.

Let's say a team has been made up of insiders, outsiders and consultants. How are the consultants rewarded? More often than not they have an interest in either the project or programme being extended (more consulting is better than less), and they may too have an interest in a particular outcome (for example, other employees in their company might benefit if a technology is chosen, or if the consulting company is selected for a follow-on project). The economics of consultancies and agencies is often based on the strategy part of projects breaking even to produce profits in the production phase. If there is no production, there may be no profit incentive. Agencies then are naturally biased to encourage their clients to put their ideas into an expensive design and build process employing tens more staff than were involved in the initial stages.

It is very important to be aware of such biases and inclinations before building teams with consultants in, much as their presence can often be very valuable.

The message, internally, should be that insiders have been seconded to innovation projects on their merits — that is, they have certain skills and knowledge.

It is also important to emphasise that those chosen to work on innovation projects have been selected, in part at least, because of their behaviours — openness, honesty, integrity and the ability to operate in a team. These behaviours are vital to the team; members who do not exhibit them should not be recruited, and in modelling the behaviours we can only hope to improve the quality of candidates in the future.

7.1.5 Do something

Compelling, if blindingly obvious, advice is that the team must get on with doing something and in doing so should make some progress on the idea. As soon as possible they should get their hands dirty learning from doing, not from philosophising.

The temptation to avoid action is high. At every turn, we will find plenty of good reasons why we should do nothing. Perhaps another company has attempted the same endeavour and declared it a failure. Perhaps a competitor is sniffing around it now — so we're too late already.

Humorist Ze Frank popularised the term 'brain crack' to refer to the concept of keeping ideas in your head so that they can avoid suffering from the disappointment that ideas tend to attract in the real world:

'I run out of ideas every day! Each day I live in mortal fear that I've used up the last idea that'll ever come to me. If you don't wanna run out of ideas the best thing to do is not to execute them. You can tell yourself that you don't have the time or resources to do 'em right. Then they stay around in your head like brain crack.'

No matter how bad things get, at least you have those good ideas that you'll get to later.

'Some people get addicted to that brain crack. And the longer they wait, the more they convince themselves of how perfectly that idea should be executed. And they imagine it on a beautiful platter with glitter and rose petals. And everyone's clapping for them. But the, but the, but the, but the bummer is most ideas kinda suck when you do 'em. And no matter how much you plan you still have to do something for the first time. And you're

almost guaranteed the first time you do something it'll blow. But somebody who does something bad three times still has three times the experience of that other person who's still dreaming of all the applause. When I get an idea, even a bad one, I try to get it out into the world as fast as possible, 'cause I certainly don't want to be addicted to brain crack.'[31]

How real is this motivation in business?

The idea of 'brain crack' might help to explain why so many of the best ideas of your business have been heard 100 times but no one has ever acted upon them. In many companies a kind of corporate brain crack is perpetuated by neither admitting any kind of failure nor being transparent about the whole process of selecting and evaluating ideas.

The main thing is to do *something* and at least make some progress, for good or for bad. The point of the process is that we know all of our ideas are pure speculation and the intended target audience no more than guesswork.

We could keep guessing 'til the cows come home, or we could start eliminating some of the guesses... which is what we should do next.

So, when we were working on Buzz Gloves, we picked cyclists as the first test market. We heard quite a bit of armchair philosophising about how cyclists weren't the right choice, they already had good alternatives etc. But ultimately, we could theorise forever, and probably scrub out each potential market that way. We were better off sticking with cyclists and learning something rather than doing nothing at all.

Now that you're committed to doing something, do yourself a favour and do it quickly. Although lean product development isn't explicitly

---

31   Frank, Z. 2006. 'Best of the Show — Brain Crack (Explicit Version)', http://www.youtube.com/watch?v=0sHCQWjTrJ8 (Warning: Link contains explicit language).

about being fast, if you reduce the amount of waste and inefficiency then you will be a lot faster to get to a better end result.

Virtually every element of our prescription delivers faster progress than the alternatives. Better proposition development may take some time in the preparation, but will actually shorten the overall product lifecycle. It will clarify and focus the build stage, making it deliver better and, more likely, on time. Experimenting gets answers faster than building full launch products. Understanding consumers through real exposure is faster and more reliable than long-winded focus groups, or even building fully-fledged prototypes.

Why be fast? Well, mostly because we hate wasting time. Time wasted on drawn out and unnecessary tasks is toxic; it encourages innovation teams to feel that the whole project is a waste of time and it makes people lazy. The measure of much of our activities during our work at Fluxx, is 'Did everyone invest their time well? And did we make good progress in good time?'

Of course, there is a business implication too. The faster a product is brought to market, the less likely it will be beaten by a competitor and the more likely the analysis of the market will remain true.

So be as quick as you can, without missing out any of the important stuff.

Chapter 8

Running an
Innovation Process

8.1 Set the project up right internally

A rguably the hardest part of running a successful innovation process is helping senior executives to understand why they should back you when you can't promise anything in return. For all the reasons we have described, this will not be usual territory for your boss. But then neither is what you are trying to achieve.

There are some strong cases to be made: most of the biggest and most valuable innovations of the past 150 years — the aeroplane, the MRI scanner, the television, PCs, social networks, the internet and

119

so on — were not created with profit in mind. And let's not forget that innovation projects that are run with targets front and foremost rarely meet those milestones (or indeed success by any other measure). That said, many total failures have also been generated by projects set up without clear targets. The challenge will be that you are likely to be competing for funding against projects that *are* promising a healthy ROI, even if they stand no better chance of delivering it than you do.

But you have one trick up your sleeve. And that is that you should not be asking for very much money. Ask for enough to get you through one or two cycles, where a cycle is enough to try something and learn something. Why would you ask for two and not one at a time? Purely because the process of asking can sometimes be unhelpfully dragged out, and asking for two at a time can, therefore, be more efficient. If the first proves that the idea won't survive, then clearly the second tranche should not be carried out anyway.

The expectation held by senior management needs to be in line with the expectation held by your team. In other words, that proposition development should precede product development, that some ideas will work but that many won't, and that the execution of a particular idea may need to change direction several times before a winning proposition is identified.

And the magic formula for doing that is... no, sorry we don't have a magic formula. We know it's possible, though, because we've done it a number of times with some of the biggest companies and brands in the UK. And each time it has been quite different.

At the simplest level, you can appeal to executive team members who know from experience that the alternatives will likely achieve nothing, and do so on the back of big failed promises which simply make everyone involved look bad. If they know what the alternative looks like, they may be more inclined to try this new approach.

It can help, too, if you can attach it to part of a trend or movement. We've mentioned Eric Reis's book *The Lean Startup* a number of times and it is certainly helpful that this has earned a huge following and has received mainstream validation and approval from sources such as the *Harvard Business Review*. The brilliantly conceived 'Preto-type' movement has also built mainstream support for experimentation-based approaches whilst acknowledging that many of the techniques have been around for a number of years.

Clearly, it will require a kind of cognitive flexibility to accept that non-predictive product development techniques are actually tried and tested whilst still accepting that they carry no guarantees of success.

But beware. The temptation to revert to more traditional programme approaches will be everywhere. When difficult questions are asked and easy answers present themselves, the temptation will be strong. But no matter how hypothetical a prediction may be made to sound — 'Let's just say… if it were to be successful, what sort of a return could we expect?' — don't mistake the appearance of a target as it hurtles towards you. Get used to saying 'I have no idea what the outcome will be, but I can explain to you how we plan to learn more about it'.

The team will need to have a wide range of skills and, if possible, should come from across the business. But more important will be the full-time availability of the team, if only for a few weeks initially.

As discussed earlier, the team should also not be incentivised for the learning project to last longer than it need be or, alternatively, being hurried through.

Checklist for moving on to the next stage:

- Executive support for the innovation programme on the understanding that it will be purely exploratory until it has created a clear product definition.

- Agreement that budget will be green lighted based on the presence of learning and the absence of showstoppers.
- Enough budget for one or two cycles of experimentation and learning.
- Full-time staff allocated to the project for a fixed time frame, with clear plans for how the team will return to their day jobs when the project is completed.
- A clear and decisive project leader, skilled in the methods we are describing.
- No executive intervention during the cycles themselves.

8.2 Strategy and context

But where do you start? What legwork is required before you even get a lean innovation unit up and running?

Whenever we start working with a new customer, we like to get a clear understanding of the markets they are currently operating in and their current strategy for moving forward. We may not be in the business of tuning or developing the *performance engine*, the money-making machine which powers the current business, but we are keen to understand its dynamics. What levers does the business seek to move on a weekly, quarterly and annual basis? What are their current opportunities for growth?

More often than not, the market for the potential revolutionary innovation adjoins the company's current market in one way or another. And so any existing information about operating in the current market is highly relevant.

A clear view of where a business is heading will also give us insights into how decisions are currently made. Quite often, existing strategy amounts to little more than 'do the same thing, make more money', either through doing a bit more of it or by improving margins. Also common are models which — explicitly or implicitly — manage the steady decline of a business by moving towards cost-cutting and margin improvement rather than growth just as a market opportunity decreases.

What is more useful is if the business in question can tell us about any changes they are considering making to their consumer proposition or delivery in order to improve either customer experience or margin. A more developed future plan of this sort can also help us understand where the new product fits into a longer-term road map.

Companies are also often able to offer significant insight into the behaviour of customers or have good research facilities that allow easier insight and access to customer groups.

Where such groundwork is clearly documented, the innovation team needs to arrange to collate and understand all of these existing materials and speak directly with the strategy or research team to understand the material in more depth. Where they don't exist, a simple context- and strategy-setting phase is very useful, even if it is the result of just a few days' work.

No company we've ever met admits to not having a strategy, but it's reasonable to ask for a few days in which teams can bring together all their strategic thinking in one place. It would be wise, for example, to speak with senior executives to discover their views of the future, as well as understanding the current challenges facing the business. This can normally be accomplished with a series of short interviews, and, depending on the questions asked, can reveal a lot to both the innovation team and the leadership team members. Asking what contentious issues consistently come up for discussion at leadership level often delivers a lot of insight. It is also very valuable to have senior executives speak about previous attempts to do new things and how they fared.

Read between the lines of what they are saying. If a previous project leader is described as 'difficult', ask yourself whether you think that person asked too many questions of senior management, or too few. Why did previous attempts fail?

Meetings with senior executives should not be wasted. While the interviewee should be the one speaking for the majority of the time, this may be your best opportunity to start sowing the seeds for how innovation will work. That said, allow them to be the ones making the suggestions. Imagine a conversation about a previous project where the budget was pulled because early returns weren't good enough. Ask whether more could have been learned if less had been risked, or whether the project should have been measured on return so early.

When you come to suggest an approach based on learning, executives who've recently been considered failures because of the predictive method will be more willing to try something new. If they believe that a more experimental approach is their idea, you have done your job very well. Don't attempt to take credit for ideas that executives steal from you. Humility is a key character trait for the good innovator.

Where research, market segmentation, customer studies or market performance reports exist, think about how this collateral can help you answer your questions. Ninety per cent of the research from your business (or external sources) may prove unhelpful, but the last thing you want to do is go out and reinvent the ten per cent which helps you answer questions.

Checklist for moving on to the next stage:

- You understand the current market.
- You have a clear view on a future business trajectory and can share this with others. The same view is shared by those who will influence the innovation stream.
- You can create a clear story for what is going to be different in this new programme.
- Senior stakeholders have a vested interest in your success and feel that they've helped create the programme.

- You have access to any interesting customer research and other analysis work carried out to date.

8.3 Building belief

When we work with clients, one of our primary tasks is to build a sense of belief. Belief in the programme, belief in individuals who are going to participate and support, and belief from the management team. As an area of focus this can persist throughout lengthy projects, even as clients prepare to take products to market or understand the implications of a product launch. But it is especially true at the start of the process.

Before we start working with clients, we often hear the most depressing accounts of previous innovation schemes, projects and initiatives. These stories can make the account we've shared in Chapter 4 seem like a week in the Caribbean.

What remains is a pathological aversion to the apparent riskiness of the whole endeavour. No longer does the concept of doing something new seem either terribly likely to succeed nor does it appear entirely safe to get involved with. 'Getting stuff done round here,' we hear, 'is extremely time-consuming. XYZ department is very slow / obstructive / unhelpful' and so on. So, if you're actually going to *do* anything, as opposed to simply musing about it, it seems like you're going to need a pretty big budget.

This is no good at all, because to get stuff done in large companies, we must spend as little money as possible, tangle with as few of these sectarian forces as we can and get output as early as possible. This is how belief is built — one step at a time.

We also need to set the stage for what is to come — we need to start teaching people straight away that most experiments will not produce expected outcomes but they will produce a great deal of learning nonetheless.

We use a variety of rapid techniques to do this, but one that's really captured the imagination of many companies is our Rapid Start event.

We looked at the typical life cycle of a product development lab (described later) and compressed it to make it fit within a time frame more normally associated with a business trip or a team trip away to review annual budgets.

Within our 'lab' environment, we had already reduced the cycle time down to one week for some projects, and part of getting ready for this is getting people used to the idea and build the confidence required to work at pace.

So we wanted to do something much faster than this. What was the shortest period that we could generate value (learning) whilst considering the logistics of bringing together influential people in our client's organisation? We settled on two days.

Within those 16 or so working hours, our teams shortlist ideas (within the first 90 minutes), develop the ideas into marketable propositions and test-market the ideas in some way, as well as examining business viability and — where necessary — feasibility.

The reaction to these experiments has been dramatic. The world-weary bunch who turn up on day one have little faith that they will be able to achieve much during the sessions. Typically they will feel they know the 'drill', having been involved in motivational brainstorms and the like in the past. They are normally surprised that we spend so little time on idea-generation, and are surprised again at how hard we want them to work, often needing to flex muscles that may not have been exercised for quite a while. For one firm, we were in the street conducting customer interviews by 11am on the first day. This was certainly not a standard day for the participants.

Aside from encouraging people out from behind their desks and their comfort zones, these experiments reveal that many of the supposed *blockers* to getting new ideas off the ground are a kind of fictional constraint — a passing of the blame parcel that is both convenient and expedient in political organisations where the focus is, and should be, on the business of today. The teams quickly see that having the ideas is not the hard part of the process. Instead it is the development, refinement and assessment of the idea which adds value to the business.

When organisations can see how much can be achieved in terms of revolutionary innovation over just a few hours, we start to break down the barriers to investing small amounts of time in working with ideas — and we increase team members' self-belief that these things can be achieved in their organisations.

Yes, there will always be risk, but if we can prove to the business that we are not risking much and that we will learn, and learn quickly, the risk becomes much more acceptable.

Checklist for moving on to the next stage:

- We have proven to the team that we can generate ideas and turn them into something valuable in just a few days.
- We have modelled a positive attitude to the negative outcome of experimentation.
- We have generated evidence that lean innovation can actually work in the organisation.
- We have a group of people who are excited and keen to participate.

Opening the doors at the Royal Opera House
(watch the video: http://vimeo.com/77413234)

The Royal Opera House (ROH) is an iconic building at the heart of London's world-famous Theatreland. Home to the Royal Opera and the Royal Ballet, the ROH is constantly seeking to engage more people in opera and ballet, and must also find new ways to raise revenue to support its ongoing activities.

As part of a Fluxx Rapid Start event, we worked with the ROH to see if we could generate two marketable propositions in just two days. What was unique about this challenge was that at the end of the 48-hour period, the team had to present their findings to a 100-strong invited audience at a venue in central London. Some people call this 'putting your money where your mouth is' as it truly was a statement of confidence that the format would deliver results!

No matter how many Rapid Starts we had run before, the extra pressure of such a major set-piece ending certainly proved a little scary to us and very motivational to the participants as, with an element of theatre, we revealed the fact just six hours before.

In order to maximise the time to work on the propositions, the teams had to settle on the ideas they would pursue in the first hour of the first day. Interestingly, neither team started out with an entirely new idea, although both were ideas which — in one form or another — had been floating around inside the ROH for several years (see 'Brain Crack', above), but had never been turned into fully fleshed-out propositions. The aim of the next two days, therefore, was not to generate more ideas but rather to convert well-liked ideas into action.

During the two days, the teams iterated business models, created live prototypes, generated customer feedback, examined the technical feasibility and cost of the services and honed their pitches.

They delivered pitches on two ideas: one focusing on new commercial partnerships and revenue streams for an opera experience at home; and the other on developing a subscription app service for ballet-led fitness.

It turned out that one of the senior directors of the ROH had a team working on a similar idea already. At the end of the 48 hours he said that more had been achieved in the two days than his team had achieved in the previous twelve months. At Fluxx, we hear comments like these over and over again after these kinds of belief-building exercises.

8.4 Create valuable ideas

Sir Ken Robinson has a fascinating definition of creativity:

> *'Imagination is not the same as creativity. Creativity takes the process of imagination to another level. My definition of creativity*

is: the process of having original ideas that have value. To be creative you actually have to do something. It involves putting your imagination to work to make something new, to come up with new solutions to problems, even to think of new problems or questions... You can think of creativity as applied imagination.'[32]

Of course, ideas for business are straightforwardly an example of creativity. Or, as Ken Robinson has it; applied imagination.

The trick for us, as it is for Sir Ken, is to ensure that the ideas we're creating have value: value for the business *and* the consumer. We already know the idea will have value for someone — specifically the person who thought of it. There's a reason why an inventor will often describe their idea as their *brainchild*. And as any parent will know, there's no such thing as an ugly baby, so long as it's your baby. Ideas can be the same. So, in fact, we need to do two things: first, strip the idea of the inventor's value; and second, assess how valuable it is to the business.

The actual creation of ideas, aka imagination — often regarded as the heroic element of new businesses — is in many ways the easiest part, and it's one which is well understood, if not very closely observed. In his 1965 book, *A Technique for Producing Ideas*,[33] James Webb Young explains more or less all of the techniques needed to go about generating ideas. And he does it in just 40 pages. So if you're not sure how to generate ideas, you could do a lot worse than reading Young's book, just as millions of other creative people have done in the last half a century.

In no time, you'll have the participants gathered and whiteboard markers, Post-its and sharpies in hand. But when you do, remember to set a clear brief. All too often, we've seen brainstormees set free with a

---

32 Robinson, K. and Aronica, L. 2009. *The Element*. London: Viking Penguin.
33 Webb Young, J. 2003. *A Technique for Producing Ideas*. New ed. New York: McGraw-Hill Advertising Classics.

remit to think 'big', 'outside the box' and so on. Narrowing the domain will produce better ideas which better meet the needs of your business.

When we are creating ideas for *things* that a business might go on to produce, we will also need to quickly evaluate that idea to see if it might be a reasonable commercial success. To do that we must strike a careful balance between only favouring ideas which are very close to the business we already understand, and taking off into wild flights of fantasy that would operate in markets we'll find hard to understand.

The first test for ideas may be surprising and, although a blunt tool, it is effective in finding that space between too easy and too hard. For those who've developed ideas, we simply ask them to choose which ones they like the most. When they know that the next step will be to develop the idea out, at which stage they will be presenting and defending their idea to the group, participants tend to quickly pick out the ideas they think most practical.

Checklist for moving on to the next stage:

- A list of ideas or high-level initiatives that have potential value.
- A group of people that are excited by, and believe in, some of those ideas.

8.5 Manage a portfolio of ideas

Let's say I work in a large international consumer packaged goods company and a few formats have been tried for new deodorants. The Australian team comes up with an idea for cat deodorants. Sounds crazy? Well, there are a lot of pet lovers out there with smelly felines and significant disposable income. And so the idea is tried and it fails. The product doesn't sell. What should happen next?

All too often the corporate instinct is that the idea should be kept secret. When development first starts, the desire is to protect our groundbreaking innovation. As we proceed and start to see the results of the trials, early sales, and so on, we decide numbers should be kept to the product team — others wouldn't understand the various subtle nuances. And then the project fails and the product line is discontinued, and nobody wants to talk about it.

What's the problem here? As George Santayana said: 'Those who cannot remember the past are condemned to repeat it.'[34] And so, in a few months, across the other side of the world, the team in the UK spend a lot of time thinking about cat-odour-related products. Or someone back in the Australian office spends time researching a dog breath product — 'Stinkies'. A lot more wasted time, finding out the same things again and again.

But that is only half the problem. Ask around the Australian team about what happens with new ideas. What will you hear? 'We often start on things but then it normally goes quiet'; 'Lots of brainstorms but nothing ever really comes of it'. Why is it that we think that our otherwise intelligent members of staff are unable to deal with the concept that we tried something and it didn't work out? Why are we afraid to go back to them to tell them we valued their thinking, but it didn't work out on this occasion?

So, we should keep a log our all the ideas we have tried and share it with anyone who is interested. It should be as detailed as possible in terms of describing what happened, and who to talk to if you want to find out more. Should we spend as much time on products that didn't work? In fact, we can afford to spend more, since the products that succeed will be known about anyway and don't need to be explained. What about the experiments that produced negative outcomes for the product's success? Share those too, and give hope to the next generation of product developers. Let them see that the road to a successful project is rarely free from obstacle and setbacks.

---

34   Santayana, G. 1905. *Reason in Common Sense*. New York: Scribner, p.284.

And what if another team has tried your idea before and failed to make it work? Does that mean you shouldn't give it a go? Not at all. But it will give you some pretty big questions to challenge. If you are to succeed where they failed, you will need to be able to work out why. Perhaps Minty Dog biscuits will work only in the Middle East. Or perhaps you have found a whole new way of selling smelly-kitten-trousers to the OAP market. It doesn't matter what it is, but if you can save time, with research already done, you can invest more in removing the assumptions which have not yet been addressed.

8.6 Build around propositions

Think of ten ideas.

Done?

Odds are that'll take you about five minutes, especially if the types of ideas you want are closely defined.

Now write a paragraph explaining each idea.

That's a bit more time-consuming. It's stopped feeling like a game and started feeling a little bit like work.

Keep the momentum up by quickly producing increasingly well-developed versions of the proposition. Bear in mind that in each iteration you are not just focusing your lens on an already complete thought but, rather, developing the idea. It might feel as if you are merely rearranging words, but what you are actually doing is changing the meaning of the proposition in each turn, and hopefully improving it, but certainly moving it along so that it can be improved at some stage.

We ask that each idea be turned into the simplest of propositions, a 'value hypothesis' or 'why would anyone want it?'.

1. **Customer.** Who are the customers you are creating this for? Is it 30-year-old mums in the south of England? Fifty-year-old

single men in France? Kids with an interest in technology? The product has to have an audience.

2. **Problem.** What problem do the customers have that you are trying to solve? Be aware of the fact that your customers may not know they have a problem now, even though they might one day be unable to live without your product — think iPod, dishwasher, smartphone, and so on. In this scenario, you might choose to position your idea as an opportunity rather than a solution to a problem. The smartphone, doesn't 'solve a problem' per se but it does exploit an opportunity 'to enhance people's access to information and content on the move'.

3. **Solution.** The very pithiest description of your answer to their problem: for example, 'store entire music collection in your pocket'. Wiring diagrams are not required in proposition statements. We don't need to know whether storage is on magnetic disc or solid state. We just need to know what it does for the consumer.

4. **Alternatives.** Are there any alternatives currently available? What do consumers do today to solve the problem?

5. **Advantages.** Why is your solution better than the alternatives?

6. **Commercial opportunity.** How will you make money out of solving the customer's problem?

A small group can typically create a draft proposition statement for an idea in just a few minutes. Yet big businesses have been built on less understanding than you will gain if you can get these simple proposition statements right.

You may also find yourself suddenly blocked by something which hadn't previously seemed important. For example, do you really understand what the competitive landscape is like, or how rival firms solve customers' problems?

If ideas are the input to this process, the key outputs — in addition to the beginnings of a defined proposition — are assumptions and, therefore, questions. Is the problem you have identified genuinely worrisome for the customer? How successful are the alternatives? What are the attitudes to them in reality? Are there enough people in the world who really match your customer profile? Is your potential customer really willing to pay what you think they will pay? Stand back from your proposition and ask yourself; how realistic is this picture? Have I invented the Segway,[35] or something like it? Now, and not after all the money stuff, is the time to get to grips with the proposition.

Let's look at a product that could have benefited from this initial review, Microsoft Zune:

1. **Customer.** Music fans.
2. **Problem.** Not being able to take their music collection with them when they are not at home.
3. **Solution.** It allows their whole collection to be stored on a small portable device.
4. **Alternatives**. Apple iPod.
5. **Advantages.** None. It is less well known, has a less vibrant ecosystem and is otherwise undifferentiated.
6. **Commercial opportunity.** Significantly less than the Apple iPod, which already has a big chunk of the market.

And a product that is successful, Google AdWords:

1. **Customer**. Existing advertisers, and companies who hadn't previously advertised because it was too expensive.
2. **Problem**. Expensive media is often not seen by those interested in buying products.

---

35 http://hbr.org/2011/04/why-most-product-launches-fail/ar/1

3. **Solution**. Ability to target those specifically searching for a product or solution.
4. **Alternatives**. Media spend across specialist websites or print titles.
5. **Advantages**. It is more immediate and precise; it can be bought in smaller units.
6. **Commercial opportunity**. The value of the entire traditional media industry, and more!

From just this simple analysis, we will focus our attention on who matters most to our business. This may seem obvious in retrospect but can be confusing at first. Note that we haven't even mentioned consumers as part of the Google AdWords case. In fact, when you're trying to understand a platform (and many models have platform elements), you will need to think separately about the two sides of the platform: advertisers and searchers in Google's case.

In six questions, we have started to think about who our most important audience is, why we matter to them, who our competitors are, and how much we might be able to charge for our product (clue: often this is zero).

By starting to create a simple model of how large an audience is, and how much they might be willing to pay, we are halfway to creating our revenue case. Now an initial estimate of costs will give us a first indication if we have a viable business on our hands.

But what if we don't? First, don't panic. In the rollercoaster of idea development, this can be a low point. But many successful business owners will tell you that this was the revelation that led them to their real breakthroughs; it was this adversity which, in fact, set them on the road to discovering the true meaning of their idea. Like so much of what we will discuss, the drafting of a plan, using Excel, using the business model canvas we discussed earlier,[36] using the back of a cigarette packet or whatever — it is an experiment. And experiments produce learning, and not money.

If the first draft doesn't work, focus on what will need to change to make the idea successful. Do we need to rethink the customers, the problem, the differentiation, or how we will charge?

Of course, not all businesses are viable, even if they would have a potentially huge demand. That free ice-cream stand on Bondi Beach would have plenty of customers but would make no money! What do we need to introduce to make a profit? Membership, sponsorship, a price for an ice cream? Make sure you account for how your business model has really changed. Is sponsorship your model? Well, the beachgoers of Sydney are no longer your customers (some would say they are now your product); instead, sponsors are. What's their problem? It's probably got nothing to do with ice cream. And so on. Same idea, different propositions.

Checklist for moving on to the next stage:

- A proposition which you and the team believe in, even after you've been forced to fill in the blanks.
- A clear list of the assumptions you will need to validate to know whether your proposition really will be a consumer success.

8.7 Harvest assumptions

The fewer assumptions we take into development, the lower the chances that our assumptions will prove false during development.

At times, the desire to sweep assumptions under the carpet can seem integral to the character of entrepreneurs. That may work for the

---

36   See http://www.businessmodelgeneration.com/canvas

luckiest and most intuitive of them but, for the rest of us, assumptions are things we need to learn about.

We shouldn't try to ignore them. We should seek them out.

Turning assumptions into facts is the key goal of the product developer. And of course this is a process of learning.

When we find that an assumption is false, it will lead us back to our original hypothesis, and that in turn will lead us to make changes to our product, how it works, and therefore the assumptions that underpin it.

Maintaining a list of assumptions, and our plans to validate them, is as essential as maintaining a risk log during project delivery. Indeed, assumptions not validated by delivery should probably go on that risk log.

Numerous techniques exist for finding more assumptions. For example, when you are further down the road with a particular product concept, try to construct an end-to-end story of how it will be used (also known as a 'user journey'). What must your customer do first to find, buy or use your product, and what happens next? Now go back and overlay the assumptions you are making at every stage. Does your customer buy your product online? Assumption: target market is comfortable with e-commerce. Assumption: target market has a credit card.

Some assumptions — like these — can be answered easily, whereas others will require you to set up and run your own experiments, or carry out further research.

Furthermore, some assumptions, ultimately, cannot be answered. But every unchecked assumption is a strike against you as move to the next stage — a problem which may come back to challenge the overall feasibility of the project. It's best to have as few as possible.

8.8 Compensate for diversions in technology and marketing

We know that if the product is really revolutionary, it will take us out of our comfort zone, either technically or in terms of understanding the market to which we are selling. Or both.

For such new products, we will often spend as much time understanding the new market or technology as understanding the new product itself. We also know that lack of fluency in either technology or market, is a key predictor of failure. Clearly, we need to try and mitigate this weakness, by being even stronger in other success factors and also by tackling the market and technology challenge head on. But how?

The first answer is a rather unfashionable one, in the business world at least, and that is we must tackle the challenge with humility. We need to understand, right from the start, that we know little about the market for our new product. We know little about how people will react to it, how important they might find it, whether they will care, whether they would ever talk about it. Even if we know a whole lot about something else, we know nothing, or very little, about this. We need to learn.

And to learn we must either provoke consumers in some way, to see how they respond; or we must do our best to get inside their minds, to understand how they really think.

Those are our only two options. We do not believe there is a third option whereby we get the customer to design the product, or provide direct feedback on it.

8.8.1 Provoking a reaction

We've already talked about techniques where we have found out with a great deal of certainty how customers will react to a proposition by simply getting them to react to that very proposition. We have created simple tests and seen how the customer reacts — will they buy the product, will they complain, what questions will they ask, and so on.

8.8.2 Getting into the head of the consumer

The growth of a huge industry around profiling and segmentation of customers might lead us to believe that the cost and effort involved in developing such understanding will be enormous. In fact, what we are trying to do is to create something very basic and fundamental in our nature. We are trying to build a relationship with, and comprehension of, our potential customers. Through conversation and interaction with those customers, we can see clearly what previously may have seemed quite opaque. What do they really care about? Why do they behave the way they do? What are their priorities? How do they relate themselves to the brands and organisations they interact with?

Often the sources of this insight are disarmingly obvious. In many cases, opinions about our products and categories are out there on the internet, just waiting to be read. Particularly with new social media platforms such as Tumblr, consumers will often tell complex and nuanced stories of the problems they are trying to solve, and their attitudes to life, to challenges and to brands. All you have to do is read it.

Not much more effort is required to take the next step, and that is to speak directly to potential customers of your product. In these conversations, consider what customers really care about rather than what they seem to care about. Ask them questions about what they find frustrating, or delightful, sad or fabulous. Get them to talk about things they love and things they hate. Let them talk. It is only when the customer is taken too literally, or asked to don the hat of the product designer, that these interactions are wasted. We have been in endless workshops with customers describing the perfect product. First, it will have every feature they've ever seen; secondly it will be… let's see, 'easy to use' — 'a button for everything'; next it will be cheap. They will then walk straight out of our session and buy an iPhone. Why? Because they don't know what they want, and they suck at product design. Yet, get them to talk about what they love about music, or what they fear when it comes to their own data, and you can start to understand what the driving forces in your own product design should be.

And try and create a meaningful model of the customers rather than a formal design persona. Surround yourself with your customers, photos from the sessions you had with them, verbatim quotes, self-profiles they created.

Remember that you are not just looking to build a picture of the consumer's life in which your product might fit. You also want to understand what the language should be to talk to your would-be consumers about your product. How do they talk to each other, how do they talk about the things they care about? Clearly you don't want to imitate them in your brand language, but this input will be vital in understanding how your marketing will be digested, and hopefully how it will be talked about.

8.9 Adapting to technology challenges

When it comes to technology, the problem is different. There are two sorts of key technology challenges: a lack of specific skills; and a lack of understanding of a particular challenge. So, for example, in considering the creation of a new online storage service, we may not have the skills in-house to correctly plan, estimate and oversee the technical development. That is certainly a challenge. Even when we *do* have those skills, we then have particular key questions to answer. Namely, can the product be produced at all, i.e. is it even possible? How much will it cost to produce and / or operate it? Do we have any options in production and operation, i.e. can it be made to be viable by doing things differently? Finally, which — if any — of the elements of producing the product can be protected to create business advantage, i.e. is there any patent potential?

In order to refine and define the proposition effectively, we need to have at least solved the first challenge. Whether through hiring, partnering or calling in favours, we need to have technical domain experts available during the planning and definition phase of the project.

As we saw from Cooper earlier, the closeness of the technology at question, to the business' established strengths, is a strong predictor of success. In other words, a lack of such expertise is a key risk.

The solution is to invest in bringing the right people on board but to avoid getting them to solve the problem straight away. Faced with a new challenge, any technologist worth his or her salt will instinctively try to solve the problem immediately. It's the same human nature that got them into technology in the first place. That doesn't mean they will start creating prototypes or writing code straight away, but you can guarantee they will start thinking about how to engineer the end product. And often they will start thinking about how to remove all of the problems from their previous project. Thoughts — in short — will turn to devising the perfect solution to your problem.

That will be a great objective. But that can be tackled later. For now, you need the technology team to switch gears, identify the questions they don't know how to answer yet and find ways to evaluate those problems, as well as doing what no engineer likes doing to support your work — creating estimates for building and operating the platform in production. Again, beware fortune-telling. What you're looking for is an order of magnitude so that you know whether you're likely to ever recover your costs.

The building of the perfect solution can come later, when you are certain that is what you actually want to do.

8.10 Incubation cycles

We arrive at this stage with an idea in which we have some faith. We probably still know little about it and are still some way away from being able to make proper predictions, but things are moving fast.

Of the assumptions we take out of the ideas generation phase we will have three groups:

1. Assumptions about technology — can we make it work?
2. Assumptions about customers
   a. How big is this problem we have identified?
   b. How passionate do customers really feel?
   c. Are customers willing to use our solution to the problem?
   d. Do they understand it?
   e. Do they find it acceptable / desirable?
   f. How do consumers respond to our differentiation?
   g What will consumers really pay, if anything?
3. Assumptions about the business
   a. Who are the competitors?
   b. What are the real costs of doing this?

Our job now is to evaluate each of these assumptions through a series of experiments. We often describe this stage as 'the lab'. Like the incubation theme, the subtext is clear. The idea still has a fragile quality at this stage. We are nurturing and developing it, hoping to evaluate strengths and weaknesses through experimentation. The idea will undoubtedly develop as it progresses through this stage.

Let's look at an example of how we move the product forward through evaluation.

Imagine we want to discover how consumers relate to a problem. Using an example from Fluxx, we were looking to understand the huge problem of food waste. Up to 50 per cent of food sold in UK supermarkets ends up being thrown in the bin by many households. Clearly this is incredibly wasteful, both for the country as a whole and the consumer in particular, who could benefit to the tune of £100s a year if they could merely improve their use of food and throw less away — and, therefore, buy less in the first place.

It is, by any measure, a huge problem. But do customers care enough to do anything about it? And what, if anything, would help them solve this challenge?

Our hypothesis was pretty simple. We suggested that if consumers found it easier to keep on top of what food they had in their fridge, they would be able to make more informed decisions, and make better use of the food they already owned.

In some senses, this is not a new idea. Certainly the idea of the 'fridge of the future' is such an old idea that it has really become the fridge of some imagined past, belonging more with black and white television and early microwaves than our current generation.

The product we had in mind was a sensor which would automatically tell you what's in your fridge wherever you were. Obviously, this is an extremely difficult thing to manufacture, and we certainly couldn't make it just to test it. So we conducted several experiments. Two of which two are described below:

8.10.1 Stick it to your fridge

We accosted customers at a number of large supermarkets and asked if we could help them pack their shopping. We then asked those that agreed if they would be willing to take part in a study aiming to reduce food waste. To do this, we needed their email address. Nothing else. We also asked them to estimate how much food they wasted and to give us an estimate of how much food (by value) was thrown away, unused each week. We recorded the use-by or sell-by dates of all of the food in the customers' baskets.

The next day we sent the customers a print-out of what was in their fridge divided up by the days in which it would expire. We even provided handy tips and advice for what to do with the food which needed to be used up each day.

Obviously, our method was neither internet-connected nor terribly clever. It did not know when consumers had used food. And so we asked customers to cross off goods as they were used.

Well, first of all, we learned how many people actually gave a hoot about food waste. Your email address may not seem that valuable but to give such personal information to a stranger with nothing more than a clipboard and a winning smile means something. Don't believe us? Try standing in the street and asking random passers-by for their email addresses.

Secondly, we learned about what people will say when you ask them whether they waste food. We did not expect this to be an accurate picture of whether food is, in fact, wasted but rather it allowed us to understand the attitudes people are willing to articulate in public.

Finally, by following up with each of the participants at the end of the week (most food you put in your fridge lasts between a week and ten days), we were able to find out how much food the customers threw away, how this varied from their estimate, and whether they felt the list had helped them (for those who had one) and how.

Of the 20 people we included in the survey, we supplied fridge door lists to ten. Those ten reported throwing away significantly less food than those who didn't receive a list.

Our conclusion? More information, delivered in an easy to use way, will help customers to reduce their food waste.

8.10.2 Whatsinmyfridge.org.uk

We refer to this as the 'Dropbox' technique. We don't know if Drew Houston, the founder of Dropbox, was the original pioneer of this approach, but it's certainly a widely talked about example of how to test an idea.

And the idea is that you create what appears to be a fully functioning product in such a way that consumers are totally persuaded that it is real, and this way we get to see a genuine reaction towards it. Drew created a video of his product in action, syncing files beautifully across multiple computers and put that in front of the sign-up form for beta users. The 10,000 sign-ups they received convinced them that the product had a strong market.

Our approach was the same — to gauge interest by setting up a site and signing up beta users. In our case, the execution was even simpler; we set up a web page to see how many signed up to it:

Of the people who visited the site (we promoted it with Google AdWords), 45 per cent clicked on the 'I want one' button. We don't know if they would have converted into a sale — but these numbers at least give us some hard evidence as to the desirability of the product and how hard, or easy, it will be to market it.

Running a lab requires a great deal of discipline. You might expect the relatively unstructured nature of the work would mean that it is difficult to judge progress. In fact, with a small team all working at the same location, it is relatively straightforward to keep the team together and working effectively. Daily team meetings are all that is really required to keep everyone aligned and sharing their learning with each other.

Using labs to drive innovation forward

LV= is an insurance company which regularly ranks at the top of customer satisfaction surveys and has, for years, been a leader in the general insurance market.

But even a company like LV= has found that there is a risk of innovation being slowed to a standstill by a relentless focus on today's business. Head of Innovation, Rod Willmott, highlighted an example, which we helped unblock with just a few days of lab work:

'The system we call Resolv= has delivered call-centre operational benefits for LV= that can be measured in many millions of pounds and has won eight customer service and innovation awards. In fact, the idea came out of a Fluxx innovation workshop that was set up to address a completely different problem.

'We had gathered to define what we wanted out of our future intranet and deliberately included people from all corners of our business. One tentative voice on day one caught the imagination of the entire audience, "I just want to be able to share my problems and knowledge with my colleagues," and right there a great idea was born for a new way to help contact centre staff give better service to customers.

'Within the two days of the workshop we had created a prototype that let everyone see the potential value in this great collaborative idea; so much so that people who had originally attended reluctantly felt compelled to persuade their senior executive colleagues to join us, saying "you have to come and see this and the process we have been going through".

'Outside of the enthusiasm of the first challenge, the cynics massed. The concept that we could share and get knowledge from anyone in the call centre was one that didn't land easily, but a few people were so enthused and empowered from that first experience that there was enough passion to convince the doubters that we should try the idea out for real. A second, dedicated 48-hour session developed the concept, with input and shaping from the end users, our contact centre team, rather than those who thought they knew what was needed from a top-down perspective.

'Our differentiation for this product was in the fact that the knowledge in the system comes from colleagues helping each other, live, as questions come in. If an answer is not already in the system, anyone can leap to the assistance of their colleagues pretty fast, thereby hopefully creating an ecosystem that makes our new product feel worthwhile and even fun to use.

'The lab metaphor and approach pervaded throughout: small changes and constant feedback; test, learn and learn again; and keep it very close to the real users. These are lessons that have gone on to serve us well in many subsequent projects.'

8.11 Cell structures

Over the years, we have toyed with various models of setting up new projects and products inside existing organisations. We've found that there will always be a tension about how close the new business is to the existing company, and exactly how it will fit into the firm's existing hierarchy.

To date, we have sought to find ways in which a company's current team can be very closely involved in the new product or proposition. The thinking behind this is straightforward: long-standing employees bring with them knowledge about the business, the ability to negotiate its many networks, and the promise of the ability to merge the new proposition back into the parent company as it comes to fruition.

While these statements remain true, we now firmly believe that if the new business is of a genuinely revolutionary nature, it must be placed outside of the parent organisation to a significant degree, even if it employs staff from that parent company. We do not necessarily mean that it should be physically, or geographically, separated but it must sit outside many of its reporting structures and constraints.

Indeed, the language we may choose to describe such new 'organisations' will have more in common with the textbooks of military strategy than business strategy. This is not the crass borrowing of military lexicon we have seen from marketers ('targets' and 'acquisitions'), but rather how to structure units based on the learning of military special forces when creating guerrilla units or 'cells' operating deep behind enemy lines. In order to carry out an essentially insurgent activity, in a context where much greater latitude, improvisation and initiative is required, a structure external to the main military hierarchy is required.

What is created is a cell of specialists with a flat command structure, and a relationship to one or two of the parent company's most senior officers. These senior officers are very hands-off, but responsible for the overall direction and objectives. They are also responsible for ensuring the cell is as well protected and well supplied as possible tapping into the logistical and other resources of the parent on an ad hoc basis. Let's call them the 'handlers', if that's not stretching the analogy too far.

Thus the team we have set up is, therefore, autonomous in decision making but supplied and protected. A critical part of this is for the handlers to shelter the group from being blocked, or slowed, by the traditional politics of the organisation, whilst providing them the funding and resources they need.

So the role of the handlers becomes critical. They must make sure that the cell has understood its remit and sticks with it. The cell must be self-sustaining, but under strict control. They must be considered vital to success, yet expendable if things go wrong (we just mean they can be redeployed, of course, not left behind enemy lines).

Multiple cells can be tasked at the same time and different cells do not necessarily need to be aware of each other's existence until this benefits their own objectives. And so it should be for the organisation as a whole; the need to see the outcomes of the new units, without being necessarily involved in their working or their methods.

Do such structures seem excessive or counter-intuitive? Well, it's how Apple developed the iPhone. It is the structure used by IBM to transform their business from hardware and software to consulting. For sure, it is also the structure used by companies who have not found success, but our assertion is that companies who have succeeded with genuinely revolutionary innovations have rarely, or never, done so from their desks in the core of the parent organisation.

8.12 Managing up

Often, the hardest part of staying on track is telling the truth to senior people, even if that truth is something which does not sound like the sort of thing a confident, experienced and successful businessperson would say, such as: 'I have no idea what is going to happen here.'

The truth is that no one could know the answers to these questions. And the best approach is to make a virtue of the essentially unknowable quality of the work you are doing.

Practise humility, honesty and straight-talking. Gain a reputation with senior management for spelling out the reality of the situation and being clear that there really aren't any alternatives.

Deep down, your bosses will know that uncertainty can't be made to disappear merely through the setting of targets and, hopefully, one day soon they will come to appreciate your approach. But never underestimate the challenge of managing upwards in the organisation. The importance of the ability to do this is just as great as keeping your teams on track as they build out and evaluate new propositions.

8.13 Making it real

All of this will get you to a much better idea of what you should be developing. One fateful day — hopefully not too long after you have started — you will have something worth the blood, sweat and tears of the development process. If you've done it right, you will have a lot of facts about your proposition. You will be able to give real answers to the key questions and assumptions which make the idea work. Hopefully too, you've been able to learn about which elements of your project matter most to your customers and add the most differentiation in the market place.

Will this spare you the standard experience of product development: endless cycles, delays, confusion and complexity? What can you do to make the next stage of the process less painful? And do we need to change our behaviour to re-emphasise confidence over learning, and certainty over doubt?

Certainly, a different style of leadership is needed. Precisely because you have learned about the proposition you are building, you should stand up for the ideas that you know are right and focus the attention of the development team on the areas you know are the most important for the customer.

The best way to communicate this certainty is by sharing both the results of the experiments you carried out and the details of how they were conducted. But be careful to also include the experiments you carried out that didn't seem to work out when you tried them. The importance of this point is that showing your failure is proof of your honesty and objectivity, and when you present them with positive outcomes, they are believed all the more.

Try also to avoid believing that the picture of the product you have in your mind must match exactly how it will end up. Just because something worked well in an experiment doesn't mean it can't be made to work exactly the same way in the development stage.

Remember why you built those imperfect prototypes in the first place. As we discussed earlier, the details of the final implementation can make the different between a success and failure, especially when we include all the nuances of pricing, distribution, marketing, support, sales, returns… whatever factors are involved in determining how the customer experiences your product.

In advertising agencies, when creating communications, the teams are divided up between 'creative' (who make the concepts) and 'design' (who actually build the final communication product). More often than not, the 'design' teams have as much to do with a standout campaign as the 'creatives'. Every member of your team, whatever they do — be it packaging, marketing, distribution, design or quality assurance — should be able to see how they can make the product better through execution. Be relentless. Encourage them, both with knowledge you have gained throughout the proposition development and with the enthusiasm you have for the product and how it will create value for your customers. Now is the time for you and your team to be passionate about the product you are building.

As Napoleon Bonaparte famously said: 'The role of the leader is to define reality and give hope.'

8.13.1 Reviewing your journey

Just how far from your core business have you ended up travelling? Remember that it's not just the product you will need to build; it is the entire business ecosystem in which it lives. And if you have found a new market or business opportunity to pursue, it is likely that you will need to break new ground to create all of those functions, as well as the product itself. Consider whether a whole new division should be formally set up to develop, launch and run the new product. Many of the clearest examples of businesses breaking with tradition and entering new markets (such as Hewlett Packard getting into the laser printer business) tell of a team for the new business which is organisationally, and physically disparate from its peers in the existing business.

Obviously, all products are different. All companies are different. And most people are pretty different. And so the exact approach that you follow will undoubtedly be… different. We've tried to be as clear and simple in our explanation as possible. No matter what you are working on, we believe there's a huge amount of value in taking a deliberative and clear-headed approach to planning how you will navigate your organisation's built-in machinery, and loosen up the ties that inevitably will bind you to the way business is done today.

By never losing sight of the fact that you are working against the grain of the company in which you are employed, you will be armed with key advantage over all those who have come before you in trying to do new things.

More Than: Helping customers regardless

Developing new products in a regulated financial industry can be fraught with difficulty and, given the emphasis on compliance with regulation, it is easy to let innovation be stopped in its tracks.

More Than had recognised this trait in its industry, yet also knew that in order to deliver value to customers and treat them well, it had to break down some industry 'norms'.

Fluxx helped build some belief in More Than's ability to do this by rapidly compressing idea generation, proposition development and experimentation into just a few days. This was done with a team that comprised people from almost all of More Than's business, from contact centre to underwriting and marketing. With all these people in the room, the ability to propose new concepts and then bring them to life was very high. The momentum and belief created by this rapidly compressed activity led More Than to believe that we should continue the approach to develop some of the thinking that had emerged.

An experiment was quickly formulated for one of the ideas. The experiment was to take two people working as claims handlers and free them from the normal procedures and controls of the call centre. They were put into a newly-created cell tasked with testing a very big idea indeed.

What they did was to transform themselves from being claims handlers to a customer help service. In traditional insurance claim scenarios, customers essentially have to fight to prove that the insurer is obliged to give them some help. In 'More Than Help' the idea was to invert that and offer the customer help from the first second of the call, regardless of whether their insurance would end up covering it.

In a real-life example, a customer called to find out whether paint spilled on their carpet was covered. In the old world they would be told that they had not opted for accidental damage cover and the call would pretty much end there. In the world of More Than Help, however, the customer was first advised on how to limit the damage whilst the call handler went away and checked the level of cover. When it was discovered that the customer was not covered, the call handler provided detailed help on how the customer could repair the damage themselves, as well as offering the discounted services of a local cleaning specialist if they preferred to have an expert do it.

Within days, the team decided to double the number of agents working in the new way. Nigel Gosden, Head of Claims, said at the time: 'There's no downside. Our people really enjoy it, and customers are loving it '

Over time, the dedicated More Than Help cell moved their Net Promoter Score (NPS) for a declined claim — where a customer called up to ask for help and then found they were not covered — from -50 to +50. In other words, customers were positively recommending More Than even though their claims had been denied.

Fewer than 80 days into the experiment, the board of More Than decided that More Than Help should be the way in which they always handled what they used to call claims. In other words, the experimental cell had outgrown the parent and now officially became the normal way of working and could fall back into the more regular hierarchies required for operational business.

A few months later, More Than Help became the subject of the company's main advertising push, and the UK's financial regulator, the FCA, praised their innovative approach.

Chapter 9

Tomorrow

Tomorrow is a new day. No matter what you've been doing up until until now, no matter how bad you've been at thinking of new ideas, no matter how bad you've been at bringing ideas to market, tomorrow is a chance for you to choose to do more of the same — or try something else.

Many of the things that you think will stop you from doing something new aren't real. They're in your head. You'll find that out when you try. We're not life coaches but we know this much to be true.

And when you do get started with something new, you should expect it to be totally different. Otherwise, where is the fun in it?

So you won't always know what every iteration holds, you won't know if your ideas are going to work, and you won't know if people want to buy what you're selling. That's alright, you've got massive corporation

there to keep you going while you learn. You're not a lean startup —
you're a super startup.

Be brave. Remember, however good your company's business model
is today, it won't last. As an innovator, your job is to extend the life your
company has by coming up with new ways to do something that adds
value. Your idea won't last forever either. That's alright. Nothing does.

And don't feel like it's your responsibility to come up with something
which will keep the jobs of all those that work in your business today.
This might be valiant but it's not realistic. Perhaps some will move to the
new business, but that cannot be your motivation. You must be focused
on your customer and the proposition you're building, and on making
that excellent.

The approaches we've suggested here are very practical. We're not
really interested in academic theories, we just want to copy the best
of what we've seen in companies doing new things. This is good, as
universities can make even the most sluggish businesses look like a hive
of activity and progress.

So much of what you must do to be successful is to unlearn the
behaviour which will make you successful in the business you're in
today. When we find something we don't know, our most natural
instinct is to poke it and prod it to find out more. But this behaviour is
not taught in the formal and informal schools of business, where we are
shown that confidence, clarity and prediction are the only hallmarks
of good leaders.

Well, prepare to be a different sort of leader; a humble one, who
sees unknowns as interesting challenges rather than threats to their
status and image. Prepare too to work harder than you ever have before.
Remember, there are two reasons why founders always look back fondly
on their early years. The first is that it was exciting. No two days are the
same. You learn not just one new thing but hundreds of new things every
day. You meet new people, think new thoughts, and flex muscles and

brain cells which may not have been touched for years. It's exhilarating. The second is that they no longer have to do it. It's so much easier to recognise the brilliance of something that was difficult to achieve when it's in the past.

But to be successful in innovation you must learn how to maintain this approach for long periods. You must pick up the next challenge as fervently as you picked up the last. When you see one idea die, you must brush yourself off and start on the next. Occasionally, that desk job may start to appeal again.

But this is the world you now occupy — making the unthinkable thinkable.

Good luck.

References

Ariely, D. 2008. *Predictably Irrational: The Hidden Forces that Shape Our Decisions*. Scarborough, Ontario: HarperCollins, Canada.

Ariely, D. 2010. *The Upside of Irrationality: The Unexpected Benefits of Defying Logic at Work and at Home*. New York: HarperCollins.

Christensen, C. 1997. *The Innovator's Dilemma*. Cambridge, MA: Harvard Business School Press.

Clark, J. 2012. *Pretotyping@work: Invent Like A Startup, Invest Like A Grownup*. Ebook: Pretotype Labs.

Cooper, R. 2001. *Winning at New Products*. Cambridge, MA: Perseus Books.

Cooper, R. and Edgett, S. 2009. *Product Innovation and Technology Strategy*. Product Development Institute Inc.

Cooper, R. and Kleinschmidt, E. 1990. *New Products: The Key Factors in Success*. Cincinnati, OH: South-Western Educational Publishing.

Govindarajan, V. and Trimble, C. 2010. *The Other Side of Innovation: Solving the Execution Challenge*. Cambridge, MA: Harvard Business School Press.

Graves, P. 2010. *Consumer.ology: The Market Research Myth, the Truth about Consumer Behaviour and the Psychology of Shopping*. London: Nicholas Brealey Publishing.

Kidder, T. 1982. *The Soul of a New Machine*. New York: Avon Books.

Kuhn, T. 1962. *The Structure of Scientific Revolutions*. Chicago, IL: University of Chicago Press.

O'Rourke, P.J. 1994. *All the Trouble In The World, The Lighter Side of Famine, Pestilence Destruction and Death*. New York, NY: Atlantic Monthly Press.

Lannon J. and Baskin M. (eds) 2007. *A Master Class in Brand Planning: The Timeless Works of Stephen King*. Chichester: Wiley

Osterwalder, A. and Pigneur, Y. 2010. *Business Model Generation*. Hoboken, NJ: Wiley.

Ries, E. 2011. *The Lean Startup*. London: Penguin.

Robinson, A. and Schroeder, D. 2014. *The Idea-Driven Organization: Unlocking the Power in Bottom-up Ideas*. San Francisco: Berrett-Koehler.

Robinson, K. and Aronica, L. 2009. *The Element*. London: Viking Penguin.

Santayana, G. 1905. *Reason in Common Sense*. New York: Scribner, p.284.

Savoia, A. 2012. *Pretotype It* (published online).

Vonnegut, K. 1991. *Slapstick*. London: Vintage.

Webb Young, J. 2003. *A Technique for Producing Ideas*. New ed. New York: McGraw-Hill Advertising Classics.

Printed in the USA
CPSIA information can be obtained
at www.ICGtesting.com
JSHW021956150824
68134JS00055B/1756